Release Your Inner Entrepreneur

Release Your Inner Entrepreneur

Fresh thinking for new business ventures

John B. Vinturella and Ben Botes

ISBN 978-1-84728-313-9

Distributed by Lulu.com

USA books by: Ingram Book Company
UK books by: Bertrams and Gartners

To our mothers

Table of Contents

"Entrepreneurship"

is a derivative of the French word "entreprendre," which means "to undertake, to pursue opportunities, to fulfill needs and wants through innovation."

"Tell me and I'll forget;

show me and I may remember;

involve me and I'll understand."

Chinese Proverb

F o r e w o r d

Do all of us have an "inner entrepreneur?"

A Google search on "inner entrepreneur," (without the quote marks) yielded 1.65 million results. I only scanned the first few pages, but was surprised at how many books, articles, and blogs discuss the concept that there is an entrepreneur within us that is dying to get out.

"fivecentnickel.com" invites us to "unleash," and "chamberlain-hart.com" to "discover" our IE. Pamela Osbey and "nzgirl.co.nz" urge us to "free" this apparently caged quality. Other verbs applied to the concept include "develop," and "find."

Fortunately, the web site accompanying this book came up first in the search. "Release Your Inner Entrepreneur" is a must read for those considering starting a business, taking an existing business to a new level, or trying to instill some entrepreneurial spirit into their job situation.

This book works because the authors know what they are talking about. John Vinturella has 40 years experience in the business world, 20 of those running his own business. Ben Botes has worked with and supported entrepreneurs on four continents. Since age 24 Ben has started and run businesses in the call center, transportation, consulting and coaching industries. Ben combines extensive research into the psychological aspects of entrepreneurs, the coaching of start-up firms and his own experience as an entrepreneur and business owner to provide you with rare insights and guidance.

John and I go back over 20 years to when he was running a dynamic and successful distributorship, and I was directing a cabinet business. He became our first franchisee, and his vision of offering one-stop shopping to the homebuilders in the area still prospers under new ownership.

When John and I sold our respective businesses in the late '90s we began meeting regularly at coffee shops. We would chat about our activities, professional and otherwise, and highlight business opportunities we perceived. I never cease to be amazed at John's ability to convert trends into business ideas and cut right to their keys to success.

My acquaintance with Ben Botes is much more recent. As I look over his work, and coaching perspective, it becomes obvious why this book is such a success. Ben is a motivator and asks the tough questions that lead to insight into becoming the person you want to be.

Buy this book and heed its message!

Harold R. Singer
President, Singer Strategic Consulting, LLC
President, MG Automation & Controls Corp.

Chapter 1
Minding Your Business

There was a time according to the Hindu legend, when people had all the knowledge of the gods. Yet time and time again, they were more interested in pleasures of the flesh than they were in using the wisdom that was lying at their feet. (Times have not changed much, have they?).

One day a god named Brahma decided to hide this wisdom where only the most persistent would discover it. He was tired of openly giving the people a gift they weren't using. And he knew if humans had to look for the answer, they would more wisely use it.

"Let's bury it deep in the earth," one god suggested.

Brahma replied, "No, too many people will dig down into the earth and find it."

"Then lets put it into the deepest ocean," said another.

Brahma rejected that idea, too. "People will learn to dive and will find it someday" he said.

A third god asked, "Why don't we hide it on the highest mountain?"

Brahma answered, "NO, people can climb the highest mountain. I have a better place. Let's hide it deep inside the people themselves. They will never think to look in there."

So it was -- and so it is.

You have all the wisdom and the power to start creating the business you envision right now. You have all the knowledge, but you don't apply what you already know. Sure there are things that get in your way. Every business has challenges and obstacles; it's the determined and skillful entrepreneurs that are able to overcome these issues in order to create a successful business.

What One Man Can Do

Entrepreneurial folklore is littered with inspirational tales of men and woman who committed to their dreams and build business empires of note. Apart from the many articles, stories and papers written on these entrepreneurs, they all share one common trait. Each one of them became their dream.

The cookie queen

At the age of 20, Debbi had no business experience, a big dream, a recipe, and a passion for sharing her cookies. She overcame her first major obstacle by convincing the bank to fund her venture. Mrs. Fields wanted to open a chocolate chip cookie bakeshop and store. On August 16, 1977, Mrs. Fields Chocolate Chippery opened its doors to the public in Palo Alto, California. Twenty-plus years later, Debbi Fields' role had expanded from managing one shop to supervising operations, brand name management, public relations and product development of her company's 600+ company-owned and franchise stores in the United States and 10 foreign nations.

Mrs. Fields had a dream of sharing her cookies with the world. Today she is recognized and acknowledged as one of the few innovators and entrepreneurs to see their name become a product brand symbol of quality that is known and revered worldwide. More than 25 years of entrepreneurial, operational and managerial experience, all of it earned

in a company she built (literally) from scratch. Founder, baker, chief cookie lover and former Chairman, of Mrs. Fields Cookies, a $450 million company she founded in 1977. Mrs. Fields has since sold her company, which, even today is seen as a market leader among fresh-baked cookie stores.
www.mrsfields.com

Against all odds

Madame CJ Walker was born in 1867 in poverty-stricken rural Louisiana. The daughter of former slaves, she was orphaned at the age of seven, then Walker and her older sister survived by working in the cotton fields of Delta and Vicksburg, Mississippi.

During the 1890s, Sarah began to suffer from a scalp ailment that caused her to lose some of her hair. Embarrassed by her appearance, she started to experimented with a variety of home-made remedies and products from different brands. Changing her name to Madame CJ Walker, she soon founded her own business and began selling Madam Walker's Wonderful Hair Grower, a scalp conditioning and healing formula. Added to her innovative formulas, she soon joined up with Marjorie Joyner who while working with Walker, invented an improved permanent wave machine. This device patented in 1928, curled or "permed" women's hair for a relatively lengthy period of time. Together Madame CJ Walker and Marjorie Joyner revolutionized the hair care and cosmetics industry for African American women early in the 20th century.

Eventually, her products formed the basis of a thriving national corporation employing at one point over 3,000 people. Her Walker System, which included a broad offering of cosmetics, licensed Walker Agents, and Walker Schools offered meaningful employment and personal growth to thousands of Black women. Madame Walker's aggressive marketing strategy combined with relentless ambition led her to be labeled as the first known African-American woman to become a self-made millionaire.

Having amassed a fortune in fifteen years, this pioneering business-woman died at the age of 52. Her prescription for success was perseverance, hard work, and faith in herself and in God, "honest business dealings" and of course, quality products. "There is no royal flower-strewn path to success," she once observed. "And if there is, I have not found it - for if I have accomplished anything in life it is because I have been willing to work hard."
www.madamecjwalker.com

The Hip-hop visionary

In 1977, while a student at City College of New York, Simmons saw his first rap show and began promoting his own shows, as well as managing artists and producing records.

Having understood from the beginning that this new creative explosion was on a par with other African-American art forms such as jazz, swing, gospel, blues, rhythm & blues, rock 'n' roll, soul and funk, Simmons introduced rap music to the downtown tastemakers in the Big Apple.

Within a five-year period, Simmons' company, Rush Artist Management, was home to hit-makers such as Whodini, Kurtis Blow and Run-DMC. Simmons also helped mold the careers of chart-topping artists such as Will Smith, LL Cool J, Public Enemy and the Beastie Boys.

Def Jam Recordings, which he co-founded in 1984, quickly became rap's premier label and in 2002 generated revenues of $780 million. Beginning with "Krush Groove" in 1985, Simmons has been involved with a number of successful movies, including "Tougher Than Leather" (1988), "The Nutty Professor" (1996), "The Addiction" (1996) and "Gridlock" (1997).

In 1991, Simmons began producing "Def Comedy Jam," the HBO show that ran for seven years and featured artists such as Martin Lawrence, Chris Tucker, Steve Harvey, DL Hughley, Jamie Foxx and Bill Bellamy.

Simmons was equally successful in his retail and fashion ventures, including Phat Fashions, which began in 1991 as Phat Farm, a $500,000 men's sportswear line, and has evolved into a $510 million lifestyle collection.

To help provide disadvantaged urban youth with significant exposure and access to the arts, including offering exhibition opportunities to underrepresented artists and artists of color, Simmons helped found the Rush Philanthropic Arts Foundation. The foundation helps more than 50 different organizations through direct funding and has provided support and assistance to hundreds of visual artists through the programs and activities of the Rush Arts Gallery and Resource Center. *http://www.defjam.com*

Dreams are the seeds of success

In 1976 when Professor Muhammad Yunus and his colleagues started giving out tiny loans under a system which later become known as the Grameen Bank. One day, interviewing a woman who made bamboo stools, he learnt that, because she had no capital of her own, she had to borrow the equivalent of 30cents to buy raw bamboo for each stool made. After repaying the middleman, she kept only a 2p profit margin. With the help of his graduate students, he discovered 42 other villagers in the same predicament.

"Their poverty was not a personal problem due to laziness or lack of intelligence, but a structural one: lack of capital. The existing system made it certain that the poor could not save a penny and could not invest in bettering themselves. Some money-lenders set interest rates as high as 10 per cent a month, some 10 per cent a week. So, no matter how hard these people worked, they would never raise themselves above subsistence level. What was needed was to link their work to capital to allow them to amass an economic cushion and earn a ready income."

And so the idea of credit for the landless was born. Yunus's first approach was to reach into his pocket and lend each of the 42 women the equivalent of $27. He set no interest rate and no repayment date: "I didn't think of myself as a banker, but as the liberator of 42 families."

Immediately, Yunus saw the impracticality of carrying on in this way, and tried to interest banks in institutionalizing his gesture by lending to the poorest, with no collateral -- Bankers laughed at him, insisting that the poor are not "creditworthy". Yunus answered, "How do you know they are not creditworthy, if you've never tried? Perhaps it is the banks that are not people-worthy?"

Undeterred, he started an experimental project in Jobra, the village he and his students had been studying, and staffed it with his graduate students. Between 1976 and 1979, his micro loans successfully changed the lives of around 500 borrowers. But it was hard work combining the project with his full-time job as a Professor, and he continued to lobby the state-owned Central Bank and the commercial banks to adopt his experiment.

Today Garmeen Bank is jointly owned by 2.4milion of its borrowers, most of whom are woman. When asked about the secret of his success, Yunus said that the two foundations of Garmeen Bank is that the poor is as trustworthy as anyone and dreams are the seeds of success. *www.grameen-info.org*

There are many other cases of great entrepreneurs and the one thing all of them have in common is that they believed in and became who they needed to be to achieve success. The question you need to ask yourself here is who do you need to become in order to achieve entrepreneurial success?

TIME OUT! YOUR COACH SAYS:

1. Who are you currently being in your day to day life?

2. What is your dream? What stands in your way?

3. Who do you need to become inorder to make your dream a reality?

Vision and Values

Much has been said and written about the achievements of visionary entrepreneurs. To a certain extent, successful entrepreneurs of recent times lend credibility and value to the profession of being an entrepreneur. Despite the terms vision and visionary being commonly used, a surprisingly few entrepreneurs are able to define what exactly the term, vision, actually means. It is important to really notice the element of 'visioning.' Many entrepreneurs claim to be visionary but lack an understanding of vision.

Whether you are a solo entrepreneur or part of a team, an entrepreneur's vision is often seen only as the ideas of one person to which others comply. Compliance does not lead to risk taking.

- *A vision creates commitment.* I am committed to my vision, which means my vision creates focused action, which fosters risk taking and experimentation. A good example is how Bill Gates had the vision of a personal computer in every home. At the time this seemed completely unreasonable but his commitment to his vision created possibilities and action.
- *Shared vision creates long-term results.* People never focus on the long term because they *have* to; only because they *want* to. For example, Cathedral builders of the middle ages needed to work together. They often took 300 years to complete the Cathedral. That meant 300 years of vision.

Take a minute and refer back to the earlier examples provided of entrepreneurs who made it. What role did vision play in their ventures? Where would they be without this vision?

Why are visions so powerful?

Visions are valuable because they are the products of the *mind* and the *heart* working together.

Visions enable us to explore possibilities, and direct us to the future. Visions enable us to create.

Visions are very compelling, very motivating. They are not an escape from reality. They allow us to create it! They provide a magnetic pull.

Visions integrate our sense of purpose and our values with the picture of how to accomplish.

Personal Questions for Value and Vision

- ➢ What is your dream?
- ➢ Is your business an opportunity worth pursuing?
- ➢ How do you want your story to go? Thirty years down the line?
- ➢ How do you want your life to look to others?
- ➢ How do you want your life to feel on a day-to-day basis?
- ➢ What do you want to say you truly know in your life and about your life?
- ➢ How would you like to be with other people?
- ➢ How do you want people to think about you?
- ➢ What is meaningful about your dream?
- ➢ What is meaningful about your contribution to the bigger picture/community/world?
- ➢ Do you have any problems (such as medical or physical) that would make pursuing this dream not feasible?
- ➢ Do you have 'skills' that are transferable to your dream?

- ➢ What contributions will your business make to its stake-holders?
- ➢ What are *you* especially good at?
- ➢ How is your contribution unique? How do you stand apart?
- ➢ What added value will your stakeholders receive?
- ➢ If you are unable to quit your job, is your dream such that you can do it part time?
- ➢ What is the great thing about this dream?
- ➢ What does that tell you about yourself?
- ➢ How would you feel if you could turn your dream into a reality?
- ➢ Do you automatically find anything negative about this dream and if yes, what?
- ➢ What are the fears you have about this dream?
- ➢ What stops you from being up to the challenge?
- ➢ Do you have the support from others to pursue this dream?

You now have to take the answers to these questions and turn it into a vision statement for yourself or your business. If it's for both business and personal, ensure that the two are aligned in their purpose.

In the end, you want a statement that indicates a direction for the future that is desirable, feasible, focused, and flexible and is conveyable in five minutes or less.

CREATING A COMPELLING FUTURE

This format was created by Leslie Cameron-Bandler

1. Construct a full visual representation (a mental picture) of yourself five years older. It might help to imagine that you are looking into a mirror that magically reflects the future.

2. When you can see yourself clearly, imagine moving into the image and becoming that future you. Feel what it is like to be this older person that is you. Once you have explored these sensations, move back out of the image such that you are in the present and can again see your future.

3. Ask your future self what he or she wants from you now. Listen well to the answer.

4. Setting your future self aside, select an area of your life in which you are not taking optimal care of yourself (such as with your finances, housing, marriage, children, health, career, appearance, etc.). Do an assessment, both positive and negative, of yourself in this area as it is today.

5. Now recall how you were within the same area five years ago.

6. Evaluate how your behavior since that time has (for better or for worse) contributed to creating your present situation.

7. Imagine in what ways you would now be worse off in this area had you behaved *very* inappropriately during the last five years.

8. Identify what else you could have done (other than what you actually did) during the last five years that would have brought you to a much better place now.

9. Now paint for yourself two pictures of the future: the first being five years from now and containing experiences and situations that you really *do* want in this area of your life; and the second being five years from now and containing experiences and situations that you really do *not* want. Each picture should contain a vivid representation of your future self-living within that very desirable or undesirable set of circumstances.

10. Look at your desired future and ask yourself, *"How can I make that happen?"* Identify a minimum of three things worth doing to make that future come true

11. Now look at your unwanted future and ask yourself, *"How can I keep this from happening to me?"* Identify a minimum of three things worth avoiding.

12. Now look again at your desired future. Each time you engage in behavior that takes you toward it, you can feel and see yourself making that desired future come true. Imagine carrying out one of the things worth doing and, as you do, see an image of your future-self happy and fulfilled as a result.

Goal Setting and Goal Getting

Success is achieving one's goals. To become successful, goal setting is essential. The very small number of people who set believable goals is the same very small number of people who become successful. These successful people use the mental laws, which prevail, in the world of achievement to get what they want. You can join them!

Effective goal setting is a challenging exercise. It requires self-knowledge and courage. Remember, whatever goals you write down you can have, provided you believe it, you are prepared to set it as a goal, and you are prepared to pay the necessary price in advance. Unfortunately, you always have to pay the price for success in advance. You have to make the necessary efforts to learn the skills, be positive and take the necessary action. Collecting information is important; making decisions is important, but only action gets results. As a business owner, your job is to get results.

Take into account the vision you created for yourself. It is now time to transform this into strategic objectives and goals.

In order to create and achieve your goals you could follow these steps:

a) Realize the importance of setting effective goals.

You are the master/mistress of your own destiny. You can be, have, or do more or less anything you want in life provided you are prepared to:

- Set it as a goal;
- Focus and concentrate on the goal on a day-to-day basis;
- Resolve to pay the necessary price in advance.

It is generally recognized that fewer than 5 per cent of people set goals. It is also generally recognized that fewer than 5 percent of people consider their lives to be successful. It should come as no surprise that the people who do become successful are the same people who do set goals. The vast majority of people do not realize that goals are important or how to set goals. Remember that you cannot set goals for other people and that they cannot set goals for you. You are responsible for setting your own goals and more importantly, account-able for the achievement of your goals.

We know that success is derived from both knowledge and positive mental attitude. We also know that failure is strongly associated with lack of knowledge and negative attitudes. Focusing on desired goals stimulates excitement and enthusiasm, which are in turn strongly associated with positive mental attitudes. Most people are not prepared to learn more or make the necessary efforts to be more positive. Millions of us think that "education" is something that you attain at school, or perhaps at a university; in fact, very few people ever recover from the damage done to their education by going to school. Real learning is a continuous change of behavior. Winners are happy to change to accommodate the world. Losers wish the world would change to accommodate them.

Clear goals are not only the essential ingredient to success and happi-ness, they also facilitate effective and streamlined decision making. With clear goals we tend to collect the relevant information, make sensible decisions, and take the necessary actions, which achieve the desired result or goal.

In order to attain success as an entrepreneur you will need to learn how to avoid time-wasting opportunities. Procrastination is not the thief of time; it is the thief of life. When you are killing time, you are killing life. When you indulge yourself in pastimes, you are passing life. Be wise in the ways in which you use your time for time is the stuff of which life is made.

b) Be clear on what you want from the future.

The vast majority of people either don't know what they want, are too vague about it or simply don't set goals and objectives for themselves. Goals should be set in line with your values and vision of the future.

This is often in the form of a personal or business vision statement. As an entrepreneur you may want to ask yourself something like:

- What is my end goal? Define your goal as clearly as possible. Whatever your goal or the purpose of your setting a goal, it is extremely important that your goals are as clear as possible. There is the law of mental dynamics, which always determines the results of our endeavor. One such rule is that the clearer your goal is, the more likely you are to attain it.

- How would I clearly visualize and describe my goal. Be specific. Don't simply say "more sales", say 100 more sales per week before the end of March 2008. This energizes the will and helps to bring the goal visualized into reality.

Generally, aptitude, talents, knowledge, enthusiasm, commitment, etc., are recommended as the ingredients of success. But even talented individuals may not succeed if they drift, experiment or waver on account of uncertain perspective or a "vision" before them. Visualization has to be realistic and well articulated, i.e., both the goal and the blueprint of the plan have to be set down in clear terms.

Written goals should consist of the following:

- What the desired result is.
- By when it will be accomplished.
- How progress will be measured along the way. (And when it will be measured.)
- What action steps are expected to be taken.
- Who is responsible for what actions and for the goal overall.

c) Determine what you really want the outcome of your goals to be.

Creating goals without a clear and measurable outcome is like taking a trip without a destination.

With a specific outcome, direction is set and you are provided with the opportunity to evaluate whether or not you are reaching the goal. Let's call this step outcome focused. One way of doing this is by framing or describing exactly what you want the outcome to be. You can do this by:

- Stating your outcome in positives.
- If it's a personal goal, ensure that the outcome is in your control.
- Aim for a specific measurable result.
- Be as specific as possible. A clear and specific outcome will ensure an effective path to that outcome.
- Examine all consequences of achieving the outcome. It needs to fit into your overall vision.

To summarize, these are the questions to ask yourself when determining a specific outcome for your goals:

1. What do you want?
2. How might you get it?
3. How might you stop yourself?
4. How would you know if you got it?

Take a few minutes to scribble down answers to these questions right now.

1. _____

2. _____

3. _____

4. _____

d) Action planning

It is important that you are able to define or identify the steps that could lead to achieving your goals. This is why the process of writing a business plan is so important. I'm a firm believer that the people starting the business and not a consultant or business plan writer should create your business plan. It may happen that the plan, however well set, may require modification as we go along the way after due deliberation. One must be ready for an unexpected turn of events. The game plan may be ready at hand but we must be creative and flexible in approach. Firmness of the resolve does not mean rigidity or one-track thinking.

Effective action planning should at least include the following:

- Gain the knowledge. Find out what other people did to achieve the same goal. It is highly unlikely that you are the first. There will be many different routes, and the knowledge is there.

- Work out a plan. Look at where you are now, look at where you want to be, and work backwards, step by step, until you can see what the first step is that you need to take to get to your goal.

- Think of possible obstacles. Think of a few scenarios where your action plan may not work. What will you do? What will everyone else do? What are your alternative options?

- Look at the whole plan to see if all the individual steps work together. Is there a more effective way of reaching this goal?

e) Take action

This is the step where many first time entrepreneurs may fail. Its important to take pro-active action rather than being re-active. The distinction between being pro vs. re-active here is an important one. The pro-active entrepreneur uses change, challenges and obstacles to her advantage. Remember that the majority of new venture opportunities are created because of change.

A few things to keep in mind when taking action:

- Keep going. Once the initial enthusiasm wears off, once the going gets tough, keep going! No one said it was easy! This is where you find out if you are really prepared to pay the price or not.
- Keep your goal in mind. Obstacles encountered while working often throw us off course towards our goals. Keep the bigger picture in mind when dealing with obstacles along the way.
- Create a success tracking fail-safe method so that you as the person responsible for your goal can track, report and reflect on your progress weekly.
- Acknowledge success and support those who fail. Make sure you acknowledge your success when reaching your goals. It is obvious that risks may not always lead to success. Remember that failure is simply an opportunity for improvement and creating breakthroughs.

In conclusion, people who do not have clear goals tend to take whatever comes along.

People who do not set goals are usually destined to spend the rest of their lives working for people who do set goals. Note: If you don't know where you are going, just about any road will take you there!

The Entrepreneurial Eco System and Motivation

Most of you may have heard the common phrase 'you are what you eat.' As much as this may be true for our health, the fact is that we are what we think. Our thoughts are the seeds from which our reality and experiences originate.

"We become what we think about all day long."

- Emerson

"Most people think only what everybody else is doing."

- Earl Nightingale

The road to achievement starts with a goal. Implant that goal in your mind and think about it all day long. Our goal for writing this book may be for you to read it and become an exceptionally successful entrepreneur.

The principal difference between the average person and the one who is highly successful seems to be in the degree of his or her personal motivation. Motivation is the hidden power in the successful person's arsenal and is the key ingredient for success. Most people, I believe are motivated or have the potential if they are aroused and interested in the activity.

Ask yourself: What motivates me? Who motivates me? Entrepreneurs who succeed create environments that support their success.

The following seven steps or actions will guide you in your quest to be more motivated. But remember, there are as many theories about motivation as there are people reading this book. You need to find the steps that are best for you and implement those steps into your life and business.

a) Be in line with your values

Our values and morals are a reflection of our spirituality, our character of who we are. Often you may find that people without motivation are those who may not be acting in line with their values.

What values are important to you and how do these reflect in what you are doing from one day to the next? If the values of trust and caring are important to you but you don't express these in your life then you may find yourself feeling unhappy or unmotivated.

Write down the values that are important to you and look at the way that your daily actions or activities are aligned with these values. As you are looking for sustainable self-motivation, you will need to find a way of incorporating your values into your life and business. You need to find a way where your expression of these core values can be done through your work.

b) Desire

To be motivated you must have an intense burning desire to get where or what you want. At this point you need to be willing to give up who you are for who you want to be.

c) Intention

You need to have a clear intention of who you want to be or what you want to accomplish. Your intention needs to be as clear as possible. Write it down if you can. Writing a clear business plan can be one way of declaring your intention.

d) Determination

To climb mountains so that absolutely nothing will stop you, you need to be able to repeat the habits, which are necessary to get there.

e) Discipline

Whether you like it or not, motivation is a discipline. In the way that athletes need discipline to get to the top, in that same way, ventures that make it are ventures driven by discipline. Motivation is strongest when it is the internalization of your goals and dreams, in other words, when you are headed on a clear path in your life's direction.

f) Focus

You need to stay focused on what you want. How can you stay focused? What can you do every day that will ensure that you stay focused on your intention? Perhaps a partner will help you stay focused, or a picture of your dream home could help.

g) Direction

Certain people have the constant challenge to reach and sustain an optimum level of motivation, which overcomes problems and brings results. If there is no challenge in what you are doing, motivation will soon wither and die.

Another aspect of setting yourself up for success is the issue of effectively managing your personal eco system. The environment that you choose to be in and your interaction with your environment plays an essential part in your business and potential success. Is your environment conducive to being productive? Do you speak or work with the right people? Do you treat yourself, your environment and other stakeholders in your business with respect?

Time Out – Your Coach Says:

1. Are you clear about what is important for you?
2. Are you committed to winning in life and as an entrepreneur?

3. Does your overall purpose govern your actions and decisions?

4. Do you accept responsibility for the outcome of your future? Are you prepared to be 100% accountable?

In addition to the above, from many years of working with people, students, entrepreneurs and clients, in order to create a sustainable business over the long term, as an entrepreneur you need to:

- Laugh a lot - particularly at yourself. Trust yourself.

- Maintain a high standard of excellence in all that you do.

- Demand of yourself that win = win is the basis of all interactions with others.

- Treat others as you would be treated.

- Appreciate and acknowledge every contribution.

- Do not rely on hearsay. Go directly to the source.

- Speak only with good purpose. Direct any complaints to someone who can do something about the situation. Do not criticize or complain to someone who cannot do something about it.

- Become a solution not a problem.
- Do not gossip and do not allow gossip.

Other aspects of your personal eco system include:

- A strong relationship with your friends and family.
- Good physical and mental health including manageable stress levels, diet, exercise and work-life balance.
- A healthy personal financial position.
- A working environment that inspires you to create, innovate and succeed.
- A working environment that is neat, uncluttered and organized.

Beating Doubt and Procrastination

Fear and doubt play a large role, not only in unsuccessful start-ups but also in the hearts and minds of want-to-be entrepreneurs who never take the leap. The fear of failure, fear of losing what you have worked for, fear of appearing foolish or incompetent, fear of not knowing what to do, fear of being taken advantage of, fear of not having what it takes. The list is endless and many of you may recognize these fears as the source of non-performance and procrastination. It is essential that you acknowledge these fears as being present and to perform and succeed irrespective of them. Most people have a range of fears hindering their progress. It's the way that you deal with the fear that will make the difference between success and failure.

How fear may show up in your life or business.

- Your ideas are not followed by structured action.

- Excuses and reasons for non-performance are the order of the day.

- A culture of blame is present.

- Time is wasted on small or unimportant issues.

- Procrastination and time spent waiting are common.

- The entrepreneur is working in rather than on his/her business.

- People are doing just what is expected, taking little initiative, and looking to each other for day to day direction.

- Defensiveness and resistance center around goal setting, feedback and performance reviews.

- Partners or people working together are overly critical of each other.

The Hidden Costs of Fear in the Workplace

Consider the following examples of fear shows up in the workplace. How many of these have you experienced and what was the result?

- Frustration erupts as potential is not acted upon.

- Relationships suffer as those who work in fear look for others to blame.

- Mistakes are more frequent.

- Potentially lucrative ideas never see the light.

- Time needed to learn new responsibilities is increased.

- Business partners are suspicious and distrusting of each other.

- Personal relations suffer as a result of frustration overspill.

- The business becomes rigid and unresponsive as too much time is spent focusing on internal issues.

- Potential problems which could be proactively addressed are not identified.

- Ideas for new products and services are not generated, resulting in missed opportunities and profits.

- Culture of fear breeds fearful, suspicious customers who buy less or buy from other vendors.

- Business networks are not used for maximum impact, resulting in lost opportunities for new customer or vendor relationships and lost business.

Breaking the pattern

Fear is often generated, not through truth, lack of ability or facts but rather through perceptions, beliefs, negative thoughts and feelings. These beliefs are used to filter experience and it is almost inevitable that anything filtered through this negativity will end up being negative itself. While most of us continuously draw conclusions based upon our preconceptions, we're not always aware of the extent of their power. If your beliefs are embedded in fear then it goes without saying that even positive new experiences will turn into fear and doubt.

Here we provide an example of unacknowledged central – or core beliefs that emit beliefs about ourselves in specific areas. These in turn, feed back into our main underlying assumption about who we are and in-turn our perception of what we are capable of. This may sound like a vicious cycle but it is a cycle that can be broken.

Many of you may recognize the scenario described below. As an entrepreneur and coach to entrepreneurs, these issues are often found not too far below the surface when investigating doubt and fear. Scenarios such as this may, to some, seem unlikely as entrepreneurs are often seen as macho, fearless and the epitome of confidence and self reliance. This is an example of how it operated for a client of mine, who considered himself undeserving and inadequate in every area of endeavor, except in his favorite sport of golf.

In this scenario the reluctant entrepreneur in question is only vaguely aware of himself as an unworthy husband, father or entrepreneur. What he does feel is that life isn't working very well for him off the golf course, although he does not know why. There is a constant sense of tension and strain.

His core belief, which in this case is that he is basically unworthy, spreads to many aspects of his life. Let's look at a few examples:

Family Relationships

As a father, he suffers from guilt when disciplining his children. He needs their approval, and is hesitant to assert himself in his parental role. Also, he withholds his real emotions from his children, fearing that they won't accept him as he really is. Instead he constructs an artificial image for himself based upon the way he thinks he should come across as a father. What his belief obscures is that his children respond to him most comfortably when he is truly being himself.

I'M NOT, SO I CAN'T

Marriage

He is thickheaded and thin-skinned with his wife at the same time. He perceives every attack from her as a serious threat, since he cannot provide his own self-approval to counteract her criticism.

Yet, he needs her approval, and to get it he acts in ways that do not represent his honest desires and feelings. As opposed to taking disputes one at a time, he allows every marital disagreement to call their whole relationship into question.

The reluctant entrepreneur

In most aspects of his work, he stays within his belief comfort zone, which is safe but unrewarding. He has a few great ideas for starting up his own business and when asked about it on the golf course he will speak about his plans with great zest and enthusiasm. He does however not want to risk losing what he has worked for his entire career and does not see himself as a winner, so he plays a corporate game whose goal it is to maintain the status quo.

TIME OUT! – YOUR COACH ASKS

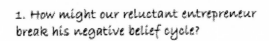

1. How might our reluctant entrepreneur break his negative belief cycle?

2. What if he stepped back for a moment and took an objective look at himself?

3. What would he observe about the way he plays golf – at which he excels – compared to the way he plays the larger game of daily life?

He might recognize how:

- He allowed himself to pursue his golf game without judging himself a failure at the outset;
- He gave himself permission to improve through practice;
- He persevered through his early mistakes with his self-respect intact; and
- He did not base his attitude toward the game or his ability on immediate results or on the approval of others.

In short, his core belief of unworthiness did not intrude on his golfing experience. He left his negative assumptions off the course, and played each hole on its merits. Challenges were taken at face value and calculated risks were taken when the opportunity presented itself.

If the golf player would allow himself to approach family and business relationships in the same manner, his central belief about himself could change or be transcended.

Shedding longstanding beliefs is a potentially lengthy process. We resist for the same reason we are reluctant to give up any habit, mental or physical as our beliefs are familiar, no matter how counter-productive they may be. Yet, with patience and a bit of determination, we can gain perspective on them.

In support of this process we can offer a few practices and techniques.

I AM, SO I CAN

One way of lifting your belief blinders and allowing yourself the possibility of clarity and authenticity is by following a process, which involves two essential steps. It is important to understand that if you have just had a disturbing experience, any accurate observations about it will be impossible without first eliminating all the conflicting messages that result from it. An initial step in this self-examination process then, is to achieve a state of relaxed receptivity.

A great way to start is by finding a quiet space where you will not be disturbed. Sit quietly and relaxed while thinking of your favorite place. This may be in a forest, your favorite beach, under the sea, on a cloud or anywhere as long as you have peace and tranquility there. The mental images, which lead you to that tranquil place, reflect what you really are about. Once inside that place you will become focused inward or centered.

At first there will be thoughts constantly invading your quietness. Don't try too hard to prevent distraction. Rather, re-direct your attention back inside your tranquil area as soon as you find your mind wandering. The combination of this re-direction of the flow of your mind and your physical relaxation will eventually cause a number of these interventions to decrease.

These meditative techniques are helpful during this first step toward surpassing your beliefs.

Another way is to concentrate on your breathing rhythms. Find a comfortable position where your back is straight. Allow your breathing to become relaxed so that it is focused mainly in your abdomen. Imagine yourself surrounded by a color, and breathe it in and exhale it until you become immersed.

Once you have arrived at a detached, calm, and introspective state through meditation you are in a better position to make clear-headed observations about your behavior in a particular situation. The meditation provides the neutral territory, which forms a backdrop for further awareness, and also puts you in close contact with immediate experience.

Now you are ready to go onto the second stage, which is to examine your beliefs by replaying the scene or encounter, which was the source of your discomfort, and to evaluate what took place by asking these questions:

1. Based on my behaviour, what was my preconceived notion about this situation or person? What filters might have clouded my perception?

2. Why did I believe this?

3. What risks was I facing there?

and...

4. What did you have to give up in order to assert yourself?
5. How could this experience have changed if your intention were different?
6. What do you know about your behavior now, which can allow you to become more comfortable in the future?

Process designed by Pat Grove

Real Scenario: **The Reluctant Entrepreneur**

Our reluctant entrepreneur is at a networking event and identifies a potential client across the room. He wants to start a conversation with her, but his reluctance to take a risk prevents this from happening.

Later we reflected on his behavior.

Q: Based on my behavior, what was my preconceived notion about this situation or person? What filters might have clouded my perception.

A: *My product might not have been interesting enough for her.*

Q: Why did I believe this?

A: *Because I have been rejected in the past and it was painful.*

Q: What risks was I facing there?

A: *My self-esteem and belief about the value of my product would have been undermined if she did not respond.*

Q: What was my intention?

A: *To get approval from someone else that my product really is valuable.*

Q: How did this intention prevent my full experience?

A: *I was basing too much of my self-esteem on the judgment of others.*

Q: What did I have to give up in order to assert myself?

A: My excessive need for approval.

Q: How could this experience have changed if my intention were different?

A: "If I hadn't been so concerned about approval, my self-esteem would have been based on my ability to assert myself with clarity. Getting someone else's approval of me or my product would be icing on the cake."

The last step in the observation process is to re-run the same scene in your mind once again. This time imagine yourself acting in such a manner that the result is a win, rather than a loss. For instance our reluctant entrepreneur pictures himself approaching the potential client confidently, letting the moment determine the dialogue, rather than relying on a rehearsed speech. The client might even surprise him by making the opening remark herself and say that she has heard of his business and was wondering if he would be here. From the conversation our reluctant entrepreneur secures a formal meeting the next day to discuss a possible order from the client.

The point is that by simply visualizing such a possibility, a whole new perspective about you has been opened up. If we are willing to allow for the possibility that things may be other than they seem, we are well on our way to taking charge of our beliefs and breaking through a self defeating cycle that may be holding us back.

Don't be afraid to fail

Most of our fears are based on past experiences or on hearsay from others. This means that at some point we created personal knowledge from our experience and now sees this as being fact. Let's compare this to the inside and outside the box analogy now so widely used by speakers and consultants.

Inside the box is the stuff we know through our experience. Outside the box is all of the stuff we don't know, but do not know that we don't know it. This is the stuff we do not think about or consider.

If we only act based upon what is in the box, based upon what we already know or which is known to already exist in the world, we will never create anything new. If we limit our commitments to what we know is achievable, we will never accomplish anything beyond the known, beyond what has gone before. Put another way, if we expect to get different results from what we have always done, we will fail (this kind of ongoing expectation is one definition of insanity). If we only make commitments based upon what we already know, and know how to do, we will not fulfil the potential that exists in new possibilities.

In other words, if you are to afraid to pursue your business dream because your knowledge from inside the box tells you that you will fail, be laughed at, lose everything or look foolish, then you will never experience your real power. This power is the power of being authentic through creating what is possible and based on the past.

This is a difficult mindset to achieve in a culture which defines personal credibility as the ability to fulfil commitments -- it must be possible from the outset to potentially fail to achieve the commitment as originally defined when it was made.

Risk taking lies at the heart of being entrepreneurial. The successful entrepreneur is the one that dares to dream and take risks. The second step of this process is to formulate an effective strategy for the transformation of this dream (or risk) into reality (or viable sustainable business). This is done via the formulation of a vision followed by the execution of your strategic goals and objectives as discussed above. Therefore, we need to get outside the "box" of our "already listening" mindsets to be able to both imagine and achieve these commitments.

The process of operating outside the box or your realm of the past is otherwise knowing and a breakthrough. Before we can create breakthroughs, we often experience breakdowns. This is the experience of hopelessness or despair that we sometimes feel as entrepreneurs. Most unsuccessful entrepreneurs will stop here and see this as proof that their original doubts or beliefs about the un-achievability of success were true. Those of us who have persevered and followed our visions relentlessly until breakthroughs appeared will know that:

Breakdowns – its part of the process

Nothing new happens until you as an entrepreneur make a commitment that does not originate from inside your box, or is not predictable, thereby creating the potential of a new and different reality.

This act of making a commitment and working toward it creates a gap between the reality of the perceived past and the possible reality enabled by the commitment.

Take the recent example of Alex Tew and his www.miliondollarhomepage. With only one month to go before he was to begin classes at a three-year university--and no money in his bank account--Alex Tew was determined to find a way to avoid student debt. Armed with a notebook and pen, Tew stayed up late one night brainstorming ways to make some quick cash.

To help jumpstart his creativity, he wrote down just one question on his notepad: How can I become a millionaire? Twenty minutes later, he had his answer: Sell one million pixels of advertising space on a website for $1 each. "I thought, 'This is one of those crazy, quirky ideas, but it just might work…I've got nothing to lose.' "

The concept was simple: Businesses could buy 10x10 or larger blocks of advertising space for a $1 per pixel and place their logos and links on his site. Tew knew no one would be interested in buying pixel space if he didn't get the ball rolling, so he convinced some family and friends to chip in to buy the first 1,000 pixels. He new that in order to get the ball rolling he would need some exposure from the media, so Alex took the money he made from the first 1,000 pixels he sold and used it to write and send out press releases to the local media.

The UK media quickly took the bait, but what was even more remark-able--and proved to be the most effective marketing tactic--was that bloggers, online forums and chat rooms also began to embrace the story. Word of mouth through all the varied media attention quickly snowballed, and within two weeks Alex sold $40,000 worth of pixels-- enough to cover his entire three years of college. It didn't take long before media in 35 other countries got wind of Alex 's million-dollar homepage idea. In just five months, Alex quickly reached his goal of selling a $1 million worth of pixels.

Millions of entrepreneurs around the world have since wondered why they did not come up with this simple yet brilliant idea. The fact is that Alex simply committed to overcoming his present circumstances by creating a new reality for himself.

This gap will always lead to breakdowns.

A breakdown is anything which gets in the way of fulfilling your commitment. If you are committed to the vision of your business that you have created then you will see any breakdown as an opportunity rather than as a problem, which in turn creates different possibilities for action. Defining something as a problem is simply an interpretation using the knowledge from inside your box.

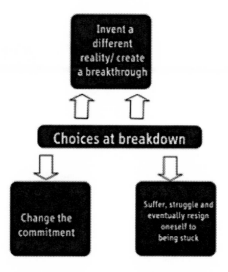

Choices at breakdown

A breakdown is essential to achieving a breakthrough.

Changing the commitment means that the originally envisioned future will not occur; this is neither good nor bad necessarily because sometimes this may result in a new, improved or bigger commitment.

Being focused on your commitments will result in breakthroughs. A breakthrough comes from being focused and asking, "What's missing?" This in turn will lead to a different set of conversations and possibilities, which lead to the achievement of your commitment.

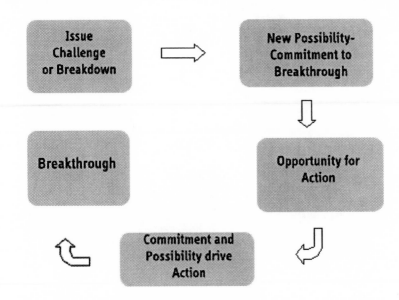

Breakthroughs come when possibilities drive commitment.

Consider the story of Alex Tew here or any of the entrepreneurs mentioned thus far, and re-write the cycle above, adding the specific details of how this applied to them.

DON'T BE AFRAID TO FAIL

You've failed many times, although you may not remember. You fell down the first time you tried to walk. You almost drowned the first time you tried to swim, didn't you?

Did you hit the ball the first time you swung a bat? Heavy hitters, the ones who hit the most home runs, also strike out a lot.

R.H. Macy failed seven times before his store in New York caught on.

English novelist John Creasey got 753 rejection slips before he published 564 books.

Babe Ruth struck out 1,330 times, but he also hit 714 home runs.

Don't worry about failure. Worry about the chances you miss when you don't even try.

- A message as published in the Wall Street Journal by United Technologies Corporation, Hartford, Connecticut 6101.

__Being Resilient__

In a recent survey conducted in support of our work on this book, a majority of the 1000 entrepreneurs who took part in a survey suggested that resilience is the deciding factor between success and failure of new businesses.

Unique Idea	9%
Owners Experience	12%
Strong Network + Networking	20%
Availability of Finance	18%
Easily Accessible Market	8%
Resilience	24%
Effective Coach or Mentor	9%

❑ **Resilience means being prepared to let go of who you are for who you can become.**

Most of us were brought up to seek the security of a regular job or profession. What happens when you mention to your family that you want to leave the security of your pension and go out on your own? They will probably advise you to be sure, to step carefully, to take your time. Some may even advise you against it completely. Are they financially independent? Did they have what it takes to go out on their own?

Are they living the life that they want? One way to avoid getting caught up in this security trap is to set a confirmed time that you will leave your job. Real worth and wealth is generated from within you. It comes from being prepared, knowing how to spot, act upon and capitalize from opportunities.

❑ Resilience means there is no time like the present

What do you want for your work? You want results. The results of your hard work are everything. You either succeed or fail. You make money or go under. Does this mean you should not get into daily routines? Of course not, as long as your routine is helping you get a profitable result, and are not considered ruts, but pathways to success. Think of it this way. Efficiency is getting the job done right. Effectiveness is getting the right job done. The resilient entrepreneur knows that there is no putting activities off till tomorrow, tomorrow will bring its own challenges. Whenever you can, do it today!

❑ Resilience means looking for opportunity, not problems

In my book an entrepreneur is someone who sees solutions where others see problems. You are an entrepreneur because others are prepared to pay you to solve their problems. Remember this is your day-to-day work and your mind set as an entrepreneur. The entrepreneurs mind set says 'what if' not 'yes but.'

❑ Resilience means keeping your eye on the bigger picture

Never lose sight of your end goal or your dream of success. Where do you want to be in ten years? What do you want to be doing? I know how hard it is trying to get the daily job done sometimes, but keep your vision alive and let it steer you in your search for success. Let it be the drive that keeps you going. Every morning before you start, do something that will bring you a little closer to your dream.

❑ **Resilience means hard work, patience and sacrifice.**

Let's face the facts; if being a successful entrepreneur were an easy ride, many more people would be doing it. To succeed you must dedicate yourself to doing what needs to be done and not be watching the clock. You must have the patience and persistence to tough out the hard times. Chances are you will be working twice as hard when working for yourself compared to any other time in your life. Be prepared to sacrifice your time and too often your social and personal life in the pursuit of success.

TIME OUT! YOUR COACH SAYS:

1. What should you be asking yourself here before implementing what you have learned?

2. What stands in your way of implementing what you have learned thus far and how can you overcome this?

3. What are the next steps that you will take now?

4. How will you know when you have been successful in implementing this?

Acknowledgement

I acknowledge the work of past thinkers, Martin Heidegger, Fernando Flores, Julio Olalla, Rafael Echeverria and Pat Grove for insights provided and used in this chapter, and take full responsibility for my interpretation and additions herein.

Chapter 2
Entrepreneurship - Concepts and Issues

What is Entrepreneurship?

Entrepreneurship is the process of creating or seizing an opportunity, and pursuing it regardless of the resources currently controlled. The American Heritage Dictionary defines an entrepreneur to be "a person who organizes, operates, and assumes the risk for business ventures."

These are rather abstract concepts for a person just beginning to consider whether they ought to start a business rather than take a job, or leave a secure job for a chance at greater self-fulfillment. Let us try to refine our understanding of entrepreneurship by asking some more specific questions.

Is everyone who runs a business an entrepreneur? What about the newspaper carrier, shoeshine person, grass cutter? Does it matter whether these are full or part-time pursuits? At what scope does self-employment as a choice become a "venture?" Is a "lifestyle" business, with no plan for growth, an entrepreneurial venture? Does it matter what we call it?

Entrepreneurship is more an attitude than a skill or a profession. We may each answer these questions differently, yet all answer appropriately within our own frame of reference.

Would you consider a person who inherits a business an entrepreneur? It is their own money and financial security at risk. They could as easily liquidate, invest in blue-chips, and live off dividends.

Would living off your success as a stock-picker be an entrepreneurial venture? What if you did it in addition to holding a full-time job?

Would a person who inherited a small or marginal business, then took it to new dimensions be considered an entrepreneur? What if that person paced the business' decline to just carry them to retirement? Is long-term success, even beyond the founder's lifetime, an important criterion to an entrepreneur?

Are franchise owners entrepreneurs? Franchises are sure things, aren't they? Is it much different from income from "passive" investments? What is the appeal of franchise ownership?

Are there entrepreneurs in large companies? How can a company promote "intrapreneurship?" Are different qualities required of a successful division manager than of a president of a successful company of similar size? Is an entrepreneur necessarily a manager?

Entrepreneurship is generally characterized by some type of innovation, a significant investment, and a strategy that values expansion. The manager is generally charged with using existing resources to make a business run well. Are these incompatible roles? Are most managers entrepreneurial?

> These questions have no one "correct" answer, but are meant to stimulate your assessing your view of entrepreneurship. This is often a useful first step in deciding whether some entrepreneurial pursuit might become a part of your career path.

Self-Analysis

Peter F. Drucker, author of Innovation and Entrepreneurship, says that anybody from any organization can learn how to be an entrepreneur, that it is "systematic work." But there is a difference between learning how to be, and succeeding as an entrepreneur. "When a person earns a degree in physics, he becomes a physicist," says Morton Kamien, a professor of entrepreneurship at Northwestern University. "But if you were to earn a degree in entrepreneurship, that wouldn't make you an entrepreneur."

What does make a person a likely "candidate" to be a successful entrepreneur? Several "yardsticks" have been proposed, but the real challenge is in accurately applying them to ourselves.

The U.S. Small Business Administration's Checklist for Going into Business suggests we begin by examining our motivation. How important to you are the reasons commonly given for people going into business for themselves? Among these reasons are freedom from work routine; being your own boss; doing what you want when you want; boredom with the current job; financial desires, and; a perceived opportunity. Which of these might be sufficient to get you to take the risk?

Personal characteristics required, according to the SBA, include leadership, decisiveness, and competitiveness. Can you objectively rate yourself in these dimensions? How much of each of these traits is enough to insure a good chance of success? Important factors in personal style include will-power, and self-discipline, comfort with the planning process, and with working with others. Are these indicators of success even for the non-entrepreneurial?

The prospective entrepreneur is led through a skills inventory that includes the hiring process, supervisory/managerial experience, business education, knowledge about the specific business of interest, and willingness to acquire the missing necessary skills. A commitment to filling any knowledge or experience gap is a very positive indicator of success.

In her Working Woman syndicated newspaper column, Niki Scott suggests questions that help us determine our fitness for the temperamental demands of entrepreneurship:

- ❑ Do you routinely accept responsibility? Are you comfortable with moderate risk?
- ❑ Do you consider yourself pro-active? Focused? A priority-setter?
- ❑ Are you confident about overcoming obstacles? Realistic about your limitations?
- ❑ Are you accurate? Controlled? Self-reliant? Disciplined? A self-starter?
- ❑ Are you comfortable accepting advice? Willing to do whatever it takes?
- ❑ Are you fair and honest? Constructive? A good delegator? A motivator?
- ❑ Are you persevering? Resilient? Do you know when to quit?

Does it still sound like fun? How does the sense of intensity and personal responsibility implied by this checklist sit with you? Does this direction still seem a few years away?

Opportunity Mindset

The process of creating or seizing an opportunity is less the result of a deliberate search than it is a mindset of maintaining a form of vigilance that is sensitized to business opportunity. This frequently relates to the prospective entrepreneur's current profession or interests, where he or she perceives a process that can be more efficiently performed an attractive new service or improvement of an existing service, or some business or geographic "niche" that is being under-served.

Successful entrepreneurs exhibit the ability to recognize an opportunity while it is still taking shape. These are often based on broad trends, which may be: demographic, such as the "graying" of America, creating opportunities in health services; sociological developments, like the "green" movement , with its emphasis on recycling and environmental sensitivity, and; cultural changes caused by changing economic conditions and technological developments.

Opportunities can also frequently be found in current and developing business trends such as the globalization of business, the need for outsourcing created by downsizing, and the burgeoning service economy. There are often localized opportunities, based on geography, natural resources, human resources in local abundance, and the like. Can you think of any for your area?

The Risk Factor

Why isn't everyone an entrepreneur? Obviously, no opportunity is a sure thing, even though the path to riches has been described as, simply "...you make some stuff, sell it for more than it cost you... that's all there is except for a few million details." The devil is in those details, and if one is not prepared to accept the possibility of failure, one should not attempt a business start-up.

It is not indicative of a negative perspective to say that an analysis of the possible reasons for failure enhances our chances of success. Can you say "failure is no big deal?" Can you separate failure of an idea from personal failure? As scary as it is to think about, many of the great entrepreneurial success stories started with a failure or two.

Entire books are devoted to the subject of why small businesses fail, but the reason is generally one, or a combination, of the following: inadequate financing often due to overly optimistic sales projections; management shortcomings, including inadequate financial controls, lax customer credit, inexperience, and neglect, and; misreading the market, often indicated by a failure to reach the "critical mass" required in sales volume and profitability due to competitive disadvantages or general industry weakness.

Some types of failure can indicate that we may not be entrepreneurial material. Foremost is reaching one's level of incompetence; if I am a great programmer, will I be a great software company president? Attitudinal problems can also be fatal, such as excessive focus on financial rewards, without the willingness to put in the work and attention required. Addressing these possibilities requires an objectivity about ourselves that not everyone can manage.

Other types of failure can be recovered from if you "learned your lesson." The most common explanation for these is that "it seemed like a good idea at the time." More specifically, we may have sought too big a "kill;" we could have looked past the flaws in a business concept because it was a business we wanted to be in. The venture could have been the victim of a muddled business concept, a weak business plan, or (more often) the absence of a plan. Sometimes factors outside our control can play a part, such as a natural disaster or recession, and may offer little information as to our "entrepreneurial mettle."

Are there any safeguards against failure? No! Even the best conceived and implemented business ventures can become market experiments that simply did not work. Our goal here is to apply a process to the planning of entrepreneurial ventures that can greatly minimize risk. That is the best that we can do, and the degree to which we can enhance our confidence about a venture must enter into any decision about its pursuit.

One of the best approaches requires patience, and to a commitment to preparation well in advance of start-up. This could be a long-range process of getting to better understand one's strengths, weaknesses, and limitations, and setting about filling knowledge and experience gaps.

We are all self-employed; even as employees of a firm, we are still primarily personal career managers. The path to an entrepreneurial venture might begin by earning a salary in the business one expects to enter, while learning more about it, and waiting for the opportune time to go out on one's own. This time can be used to develop a support network, professional and personal, and generating ideas to "bounce off" people whose opinion one respects.

Once an idea is thought to represent a real opportunity, one must be able to research the market, know what data is important and how to gather it meaningfully, and know what actions this information indicates. This can then be worked into a rather detailed plan, and then refined into a blueprint for success.

In the Wall Street Journal, Ken Elias' article on "Why My Business Failed" offers some rather tangible suggestions that could be useful in such a blueprint:

- ❑ Don't budget your expectations.
  Nothing happens according to plan; things happen not incrementally but in bundles. Sales and expenses come in lumps; in cash flow, plan for the worst.

- ❑ Beware of cheap help.
  Inexperienced or incompetent employees consume your precious time in guidance and damage control. Good employees make good impressions.

- ❑ Talk the vision, sell the reality.
  Talk about what you see in the future, but only sell what you can actually deliver.

- ❑ Even if the concept is right, it won't fly if the strategy is wrong.
  Acknowledge that it is more likely than not for your strategy to be wrong, and be prepared to change it.

- ❑ Appoint a Board of Directors for oversight.
  Your point of view is distorted from being too close to the venture.

- ❑ Great meetings don't mean sales.
- ❑ Find customers that are ready to buy today.

Elias concludes by asking himself whether he would start another business today: "Absolutely. The experience is fabulous, exciting and the possibility of success is always there. But next time I'll follow my own advice."

This advice was hard-won. We hope to let the lessons of others ease your path, and will begin with a discussion of recognizing and evaluating opportunities.

Small Business Opportunities

Opportunity Defined

"An opportunity is attractive, durable, and timely and is anchored in a product or service that creates or adds value for its buyer or end user. Opportunities are created because there are changing circumstances, inconsistencies, chaos, lags, or leads, information gaps, and a variety of other vacuums, and because there are entrepreneurs who can recognize and seize them." (Source: Jeff Timmons, New Venture Creation; see Amazon.com).

What businesses are currently in rapid change and uncertainty? Where is today's chaos? Where are our area's lags, leads, and gaps? Do we see a service vacuum we could help fill?

Ideas may be easy enough to generate, but an idea is not necessarily an opportunity! Building a "better mousetrap" does not insure success; other factors include fit, timing, and resources.

For an idea to be an opportunity:
(Illustrated by Mini-Case 1: The Coffee Shop)

- ❑ The "window of opportunity" is opening, and will remain open long enough.
    My section of town is growing rapidly, and services are not quite keeping up. "People" are saying that we desperately need a good coffee shop, and an office supply store. We cannot be the only entrepreneurs that perceive this. How long before the need becomes compelling enough for others to jump in? (Who are these people? Are they just in our immediate circle? Are they representative enough of the area to extrapolate from?)

- ❑ Entry is feasible, and achievable with the committed principals. Two friends want to be partners with me in a venture; one is managing a coffee shop across town, and willing to manage a startup. We could muster the capital for a coffee shop, but an office supply store seems outside our reach.

❑ The proposed venture has some competitive advantage.
We were among the first to locate in the new area, and are
very active in the local business community. We know of
an ideal site, and the building manager is a friend. She is
willing to sub-contract the beverage and light-meal services
the building provides tenants.

❑ The economics of the venture are "rewarding and forgiving."
Materials costs are a small percentage of revenues; site
preparation and equipment costs are minimal. We can
break even at what seems to be an easily achievable volume.

Being first to the market with a good idea does not insure success unless one can preempt competition by quickly grabbing a large
market share, or by erecting other barriers to the entry of competitors.
Could we withstand Starbucks' entry into the market?

Systematic Search for Opportunities

Where do business ideas come from? The best place to start is
with what you know. Most often, they come from work experience
and personal interests, such as hobbies; other sources of ideas can be
friends and relatives, and our educational background.

The idea generating process can be "seeded" by market research. For
example, much has been written about the U.S. economy's "exporting"
manufacturing capacity, and replacing this activity with services.
Service industry growth is good news for prospective entrepreneurs.
Service businesses are relatively easy to start, and economies of scale
are not generally sufficient to give larger companies a significant
competitive edge.

Why do service businesses seem to dominate job growth? Is it that
people today value time and convenience, which services produce,
over more tangible products? Is automation providing productivity
gains that are allowing increasing demand to be satisfied with rela-

tively few additional workers? Or is it that services must be produced locally, whereas goods for local consumption can be produced anywhere in the world?

Is there a down side to job growth being dominated by the service industry? Will we become a nation of "burger-flippers?" Can "brain-power" be a service? What forms might this take? Can it be exported?

Is there some consulting function you can perform that people need? What skills do you have that separate you from "the masses?" Can this be turned into a business?

Which service businesses do you enjoy dealing with? What distinguishes their service from other similar businesses? What lessons can you draw for any business you might start? It is not enough any more to just say that you put the customer first; there must be meaningful, tangible evidence.

"Brainstorming" and Trend-Tracking

- Earlier we discussed how demographic and cultural changes are creating opportunities. Futurist Faith Popcorn, in The Popcorn Report, suggests some broad areas of cultural and psychographic change that are creating new areas of opportunity:

- For the first time, wilderness is safer than civilization.
  - o This is creating a "paranoia" industry (security systems), fostering "cocooning" (home entertainment), and "cashing out" (moving to the country and the simpler life).

- For the first time, nature is our enemy rather than our ally.
  - o This is generating interest in "safe thrills," "down-aging" (ways to feel younger than we are), and ecology-mindedness.

- Say no to drugs, yes to "foodaceuticals."
  - Our food must feel indulgent, yet promote health.

- We all need a little "adrenaline-adjusting."
  - We need help in feeling better about ourselves ("ego-nomics") and in dealing with our frantic lifestyles; we are becoming vigilant, if not "vigilante" consumers.

Popcorn suggests that a venture that "taps into" two or more of these needs in a competitive way will be a winner. Which of these does your idea address?

More specific ideas are often suggested in the business and entrepreneurship literature; in a recent cover story, Entrepreneur magazine recently presented their view of the "Hot Ideas for 2006;" below are just three of their 29 business ideas.

The $6.8 billion tea industry is one of the strongest beverage markets, on track to reach $10 billion by 2010.

American consumers are increasingly turning to the internet for specialty foods ranging from gourmet cheeses and fine wines to gluten-free and diabetic-friendly products.

Consulting firm Frost & Sullivan estimates surveillance cameras will be a $4.09 billion market by 2010.

Other useful sources of inspiration include Business Week magazine, the business section of the local newspaper and the local business weekly. Broad trends can be tracked merely by being a reasonably well-informed observer of the popular culture.

Are these types of opportunity listings useful? Is it already too late by the time a type of business is publicly acknowledged to be an opportunity? Is it better to wait for the "first movers" to clarify exactly what services consumers want, and then enter with a more focused product?

Practical Activity 1: Opportunity Scan

- Scan the current literature for opportunities that fit your strengths and interests.
- Describe a specific business that would take advantage of one of these opportunities.
- What are your strengths and weaknesses for developing such a venture?
- What are the critical factors to success of the venture?

The Entrepreneurial Process

While the conditions under which people start or acquire businesses vary greatly, certain steps may be considered common to all:

Commitment

Do I really want to start or own a business? Am I willing to take on the personal demands of entrepreneurship?

Can I live without a regular paycheck, a predictable work schedule, and for a while without vacations and other benefits?

Is there a product or service that fits my talents or desires? Am I ready yet?

Can I muster the resources to make the venture a success? Am I prepared for the possibility that I might lose my money and property, and do damage to my health and self-respect?

For women and minorities, there are additional considerations relevant to their chances of success. Why is it more difficult for them? How much is due to discrimination and skepticism by the support structure, and how much is due to a "confidence gap" within the principals? Do they have to be "better" to make it, or is entrepreneurship the only true meritocracy? Is any disadvantage only at startup?

Selection

The basic rule is simple: "Find a market need and fill it!" The process of finding the need, and the method chosen to fill it are where the difficulties arise.

Based on my opportunity scan, does the market need a product or service that is not currently being provided? Is there a needed product or service currently being provided in a less than satisfactory way? Is some particular market being underserved due to capacity shortages or location gaps? Can I serve any of these needs with some competitive advantage?

What type of business could best seize this opportunity? Do I need partners? Where will I locate? Whom would we serve, and how? Would my chances be improved by buying a franchise or an existing business, as opposed to starting a venture "from scratch?" How do I go about evaluating the possibilities? How much study is warranted? What type of information is relevant?

Planning

Once a business idea is selected, the concept must be sharpened by a detailed planning process. The result of this step is a comprehensive business plan, with its major components being the marketing "mix", the strategic plan, operational and logistical structures, and the financial proposal.

Marketing mix issues focus on how the product or service is differentiated from the competition. A business can differentiate itself on any of what are often referred to as the "four P's" of marketing: product characteristics, price structure, place or method of distribution, and/or promotional strategy. How did our neighborhood coffee shop differentiate itself?

Strategic issues relate broadly to the company's mission and goals. Every venture must continually assess its strengths and weaknesses, the opportunities to be seized, and any threats to the success and future plans of the business.

Operational issues relate to company structure, and to the more tangible items such as location, equipment, and methods of distribution. Decisions on these issues largely determine startup costs.

The financial proposal includes an estimate of the amount of money needed to start the venture, to absorb losses during the start-up period, and to provide sufficient working capital to avoid cash shortages. It projects sales and profitability over some period into the future, generally 3 to 5 years. Where outside funding is sought, it also describes distribution of ownership of the venture and methods of debt repayment and/or buyback of partial ownership

Implementation

The business plan is the "blueprint" for the implementation process. It focuses on the four major sub-plans: marketing; strategy; operational/logistic, and; financial. Actions to be performed that are not specifically described in the plan involve finding lenders or investors, identifying a business or franchise to buy where appropriate, determining a specific business location, and conducting the negotiations and acquiring the permits required to get to a "customer-ready" condition.

We will now assume that the reader is past the commitment step, and concentrate on the latter three steps in the entrepreneurial process in the next two chapters. Before doing that, however, we will build some added perspective on the nature of small business.

The Nature of Small Business

What does small business have to do with entrepreneurship? A small business is the usual product of entrepreneurship. Over half of business start-ups consist of 1 or 2 employees. What kinds of businesses can you enter with only 1 or 2 employees? Can a person start a large business?

Only 4% of businesses employ over 20 people at start-up. What kinds of businesses are the larger start-ups likely to be?

The number of small businesses in the United States is on the order of 25 million, and increasing at a rate approaching a million a year. Why do you think the number of small businesses is growing while large companies are downsizing? Is the downsizing driving some growth in business formation?

Small businesses are characterized by independent management, closely-held ownership, a primarily local area of operations, and a scale that is small in comparison with competitors. They can be "lifestyle" businesses, where the primary objective is employment for the principals, or "entrepreneurial ventures," with a commitment to substantial growth in scale of operations and profitability.

Why do people start small businesses? The reasons are varied, but cluster around five basic objectives. The primary motivation for most business start-ups is to allow the entrepreneur to achieve independence; money is secondary. Is this surprising? What is your motivation?

The other reasons named most often are that an opportunity presented itself, a person took over the family business, or that the person simply wanted to be an entrepreneur. For context, what is the appeal of corporate life? Of a government job? A union job? Rich parents? What kind of people start their own businesses? Are skills any different from working in a large business? Do they need to be their own boss because they are social misfits, or otherwise incapable of working for other people? The opposite is more often the case.

Most entrepreneurs have similar personal characteristics, including the desire to control their own destiny. This confidence leads to their valuing control, freedom, flexibility; and self-reliance.. They generally value achievement over money, contrary to the popular notion. They desire responsibility and personal fulfillment.

Most entrepreneurs are not "gamblers;" they have a preference for moderate risk (How moderate do you think?). They are always searching for opportunities, and willing to pursue some.

More successful entrepreneurs tend to be proactive, assertive, and highly observant. They are efficient, quality-conscious, and good at planning and procedures. As business operators, they are committed to "partnership" with employees, customers, suppliers, and their community. Would these skills or personality traits lead to success at any venture? Which are vital for success as corporate employees?

Are start-ups for overachievers only? What are the chances for any person willing to work hard, set goals, and be accountable for the results?

Some of the more tangible characteristics of new businesses and their owners were measured in a recent survey of almost 3,000 businesses commissioned by the National Federation of Small Business and American Express. Among the more interesting findings were that about 64% were startups, and 30% were purchased, with the remainder inherited, promoted or otherwise brought into ownership. About 11% of the businesses operate under a franchise name.

Surveys also show that more new businesses are started by entrepreneurs in their 30's than any other age range. Why do you think so many new business owners and managers are in their 30s? Are entrepreneurs born (demanding parents, ethnic tradition) or made? Is it for you? At what age? What else do you need to do to be ready? Can entrepreneurship be taught?

A primary inhibitor of business start-up is that few people have the financial cushion to give up a job for the uncertain income of a start-up venture. Small business owners recently identified inadequate funding as their biggest hurdle (named by 31%). Overall, 28% said lenders were too conservative, 16% reported being unable to find investors, and 12% claimed a lack of collateral.

Even where the start-up investment consists largely of other people's money, the amount of financial risk for the entrepreneur is beyond what most can responsibly handle. For many with the financial means, the stress of bearing complete responsibility for the company's direction and performance is the discouraging factor.

Various estimates have been made for the failure rate of business start-ups, based on various concepts of failure and of appropriate survey methods. There seems to be a consensus that less than half of new businesses survive the start-up "trauma."

Perhaps, a major reason for what seems to be a high failure rate is that it is so easy to start a business. There is no institutionalized check of qualifications in the U.S.; on the contrary, our tax dollars fund the Small Business Administration and a number of other agencies and programs to encourage business formation.
The winners tend to be those who can find some competitive edge, even when their product or service is similar to those around them. Marketing professionals often call this edge the "unique selling proposition," or USP. Pinpointing and refining one's USP is not a simple matter. Charlotte Taylor, in a recent Entrepreneur "Small Business Advisor" column suggests:

- Put yourself in your customer's shoes; satisfy their needs, not yours.

- Know what motivates behavior and buying decisions.

- Find the real reasons people buy your product instead of a competitor's. Ask them!

- "Shop" the competition, be open-minded about your product, and never stop looking for ways to make your product stand out.

Conveying one's USP can be a serious challenge. An approach is unique only in the context of our competitors' marketing messages. We must identify what they say they sell, not just product and service characteristics. For example, Charles Revson, founder of Revlon, insisted that he sold hope, not makeup. Similarly, United Airlines sells "friendly skies," and Wal-Mart sells "always" the low price. Do these slogans convey how each company views their customers? Does their selling proposition appeal to your preferences?

Surveys consistently show the American regard for entrepreneurs; approval of a son or daughter starting a business exceeds 80%. Business owners scored first in a Princeton survey of positive influence of selected groups on "the way things are going," ahead of technology, the church, and environmentalists.
Entrepreneurship is part of our culture, recognized as far back as 1840, when Alexis de Tocqueville, in Democracy in America, said "What most astonished me in the United States is not so much the marvelous grandeur of some undertakings as the innumerable multitude of small ones."

Practical Activity 2: Company Prospectus

- Recast your business idea in terms of its competitive advantage.
- Prepare an industry analysis (size, customers, trends, competitiveness)
- Identify your specific market, and estimate the share you think you can capture.

Summary

While most of us have a fairly clear image of what entrepreneurship is, development of a useful working definition of an entrepreneur is a challenge. This is more than an exercise in semantics; for each of us, our concept of the profile of an entrepreneur can be the basis for evaluating our fitness for the role, deciding whether or not to pursue an entrepreneurial venture, and the timing and scope of that pursuit.

Unlike most other career paths, there is little consensus on how to prepare a person for life as an entrepreneur. Many feel that entrepreneurs are born that way, and that there is no appropriate formal preparation. We contend that, given certain personal characteristics, a person with entrepreneurial interest can be taught an approach to recognizing and evaluating opportunities that will minimize the risk that forms the downside of the business venture.

The necessary personal characteristics are fairly easy to identify. The problem is in objectively evaluating ourselves against measures as subjective as leadership, decisiveness, and competitiveness.

Planning and team working skills can be developed, but the same can not necessarily be said for will power and self discipline. Sensitivity to the existence of an opportunity can be sharpened, but our tolerance for risk can be hard to raise.

We can begin our "fearless" self-assessment by seriously considering the following questions:

What are my real reasons for considering going into business? These need to be strong enough to sustain you when the excitement of the startup has passed, and the everyday grind begins.

Do I have an adequate support structure? If you have a spouse, or are relying on some other form of family support, make sure that they understand the sacrifices involved and the pressures these will put on relationships.

Do I respond well to continuous pressure? Startup pressures will suspend vacations and holidays and take up much of your weekends. Even after startup, business concerns seldom end when you lock the door at closing time.

Am I willing to subordinate all other interests and goals, for an indeterminate period, to developing this business? There is more to life than work, and maintaining a balanced and healthy lifestyle can be a challenge for the self-employed.

Fortunately, we do not have to decide right away. There is an entrepreneurial process, that we are going to discuss in detail, that takes us through a series of steps that makes the final decision of whether to undertake a venture a fairly clear one. Along the way, we will develop a better understanding of the fit and feel of the actions required to our unique temperament.

The steps in the process may be rather broadly defined as:

- Commitment:
  Am I ready to deal with the uncertainty of a regular paycheck, the lack of any structure other than that which I provide?

- Selection:
  Is there a market need that I can competitively fill, do I have the necessary information and experience?

- Planning:
  What is my strategy, how will I differentiate myself from competitors, what is the sales potential, how quickly can it be achieved?

- Implementation:
  Where do I locate, do I need partners, what size and scope of business is called for, how much capital is required?

This chapter has dealt rather broadly with the issue of commitment. The following chapter will deal with the selection process in detail.

TIME OUT! - YOUR COACH SAYS

1. How well do you fit the entrepreneur's profile?

2. Is there some product or service you could competitively offer the market now? If not, what type of business might some future offering come from? When?

3. What are the primary reasons for the failure of entrepreneurial ventures? What can you learn from this?

4. When is a business idea an opportunity?

Real Scenario 1:   Used-Book Store

"We've got the merchandise and the store; all we need now is an identity."

Dwight Payne summed up the status of a new venture he just initiated with friend Gary Heap. Dwight and Gary reside in Santa Barbara, CA, where they attend college and pursue their mutual hobby of science-fiction book collecting.

"Dwight and I are really into science fiction," Heap explains. "We have pooled our book collection and have over 4,000 volumes - Heinlein, Van Vogt, Asimov, Bester, Moorcock, Pohl. You name the book; it's somewhere in our collection."

"Not only that," Payne adds, "we've got sci-fi magazines going back over twenty-five years. All neatly catalogued and indexed. I'll bet it would cost us $20,000 to assemble this collection today."

Payne and Heap decided that, at the end of this school year, they will dedicate the summer to getting a used-book store started in Santa Barbara as a means of supplementing their income year-round. They elaborate:

Payne: Gary and I figured that we might as well try to capitalize on our love of books and reading. Both of us are familiar with used-book store operations because we have haunted them so regularly in building our collection. We've been to just about every used-paperback operation in Southern California. A lot of them seem to be profiting.

Heap: My uncle owns a storefront near the University, and we made a deal for him to rebuild it as a used-book store; it's just about finished. He also co-signed an inventory loan for $4,000 for some start-up working capital. In exchange he gets 25 percent of our sales for two years. Not a bad deal, actually, since it is such a good location to serve the hordes of avid readers uptown.

Payne: Just three weeks after lining up the building, Gary and I lucked into a deal in Ventura. The owner of a pretty good-sized used-paperback outlet put his merchandise up for sale to raise some quick cash.

Heap: We swung a good deal with him - over 10,000 paperbacks, magazines, and comics for $3,500, and $1,500 for all the shelving we will need. We borrowed the money from some fraternity brothers, rented a U-Haul truck, and carted the stuff home.

Payne: It filled the building about half way. We're currently cataloging the stuff. We got a great deal. Most of the books are in good shape and recent. It's a good mixture of fiction and nonfiction, including westerns, mysteries, gothic, biographies, and a few technical books.

Heap: We're virtually ready to open the doors, but we still haven't decided on what competitive strategy to use. We don't want to be just another used-book store. There are a half-dozen of those around town. We want to be something different in our image and in the way we operate.

Payne: We want to be able to attract customers based on our differentiated image and unique style of operating. We're looking to be something a little different. And profitable!

PUT YOURSELF IN THEIR SHOES

This case is a "do-it-yourselfer." Rather than passively accepting decisions, policies and estimates, let us generate them ourselves to get a feel for what is involved in roughing out a preliminary plan.

The marketing concept

- Suggest a marketing concept for the store, including a name.
- Who are the customers? What are they looking for?
- How will Dwight and Gary meet their needs? (Company image, policies)
- How will they get known? (Advertising, promotions, competitive edge)

Reality check

- Decide on days of the week and hours the store will be open.

- Estimate staffing required and hourly salary costs.

- Do Dwight and Gary really work for free?

- What is a reasonable expectation of customers per day? Average purchase per customer?

- What are pessimistic and optimistic values of these estimates?

- How much will they have to spend on advertising and promotion to meet these estimates?

- What will they pay, on average, for each book?

- How much can they get, on average, for each book?

Feasibility Study Worksheet

Estimate the profitability of the venture. Use low, expected, and optimistic sales estimates and estimate a break-even sales level. Make reasonable assumptions where information is missing. Payroll cost may be assumed to be wages paid only. Debt service payments may be assumed to total $400 per month.

- Fill in the table on the next page, or use a spreadsheet for the calculations.
- Then, answer the burning question:
- Would you do it if you were they?

Dwight and Gary's Bookstore   Pro-Forma Income Statement

Monthly Estimates		Low	Expected	Optimistic	Break-even
Sales	-				
Cost of Goods	=				
Gross Margin					
Payroll	+				
Rent	+				
Utilities	+				
Promotion	+				
Debt Svc	+				
Other	=				
Total Expense					
Profit/Loss					

Chapter 3
Venture Screening and Selection

Before buying or investing in a business it is important to find out all there is about the potential new opportunity. Don't rush into anything, no matter how a good an opportunity it may sound at the outset. If you are going to invest time and money into something ensure that you are able to make an informed choice.

Market Research Fundamentals

Market research can be thought of as a three-part process:

(1) Determine what we need to know

- Who are our customers? Where are they?
- How are they best reached?
- What are they buying? From whom? Why?
- What are their price expectations?
- How big is the market? How much is "up for grabs?"
- How intense is the competition?
- What are their advantages/disadvantages?
- How is the product distributed, marketed?
- How are prices set and changed?

As an example of using these questions to gain greater focus and insight into a venture, let us consider a case with which the author has been closely acquainted since 1977. This case will be revisited several times within this text to build on the understanding developed, and to investigate the impact over time of the decisions made.

While the case is set in southeast Louisiana, and the focus is on a wholesale distribution business, the lessons learned are widely applicable.

Real Scenario 2:   St. Tammany Parish

> There is something basically wrong with our market research.

John and Alan Vinturella visited western St. Tammany parish (WST) in early 1977 to evaluate the feasibility of opening a branch of their family-owned plumbing supply firm based in Metairie, LA (suburban New Orleans). WST, 40 miles north of Metairie across Lake Pontchartrain, was a generally rural area, thought to have the potential to be an "exurb" of New Orleans in the future.

The parent firm, Southland Plumbing Supply, Inc., had been serving plumbing contractors in the greater New Orleans area for about 10 years at the time. Neither John nor Alan had ever been involved in a business startup, or the opening of a branch, before this.

Based on their study, they concluded that it was premature to open now. The local phone directory listed only 3 plumbing companies, the likeliest constituency for the proposed business. Discussions with principals of the three businesses were not encouraging; each managed to get what they needed delivered by remote supply houses, and local hardware stores stocked enough supplies to get them through an emergency. Only one of the plumbers was aggressively seeking to grow the business.

They visited the hardware store in town considered to have the best inventory of plumbing supplies, and these items did not appear to be a significant portion of their business. The store was buying from the same suppliers as the plumbers.

But their father insisted that the area was promising, and to re-think the issue. A "brainstorming" session led to some insight into what might have been wrong with their basic approach. John and Alan were applying their experience in Metairie to the Covington situation, when the differences rendered much of this experience inapplicable.

A supply house in Metairie, as in most urban markets, served only the "trade," that is licensed plumbing contractors, maintenance people, and public agencies. Should end users of plumbing products, or even intermediaries like builders, attempt to buy from a supply house, they would be referred to a tradesperson. In a rural market, with its smaller trade firms and more lax building codes, many people literally built their own homes, and the material was as likely to be bought by the homeowner, builder, or a handyman as by the trade.

In addition, Metairie was a "mature" market, where new residential construction was a relatively small component of supply house sales; much of the demand was for commercial construction and maintenance materials, and repair, replacement and renovation items for the area's aging housing stock. In contrast, Covington and nearby Mandeville formed a growing bedroom community, and most of the "action" was in new residential construction.

These observations emphasize that while the "numbers" are useful, they can lead to erroneous conclusions without a good feel for the nature of this type of business, and the characteristics of the specific market under consideration.
With these changes in their thinking, John crafted a new market research approach and continued his feasibility study. The potential sales volume was less a function of current population than of leading indicators, such as the rate of issuance of building permits.

Since permits included an estimated value of the finished house, and norms existed for the percentage attributable to plumbing materials, the dollar volume of plumbing supply sales in the area could be estimated. Applying an estimate of Southland's market share would then yield its expected sales volume. While the compounding of these estimates would yield a fairly wide range for expected sales, it would be indicative of the area's potential.

The branch would be basically a wholesaling operation, but retail sales would also be made. The customers would not be just plumbers, but everyone building a new home in the Covington-Mandeville area. Its product line would go beyond traditional plumbing items to include related homebuilding materials undersupplied to the area, such as septic tanks and water well equipment.

Pricing would be competitive, but the added value of being a local operation allowed some flexibility. Traditional selling, almost exclusively supply house salespersons calling in person on plumbing contractors, would be replaced by advertising in the local "shopper" newspapers. The branch would locate on the main highway between Covington and Mandeville.

With this marketing plan, John could "run some numbers," and evaluate whether opening the branch made good business sense.

 **PUT YOURSELF IN THEIR SHOES**

- What do you think of John's marketing plan? Did he show a good grasp of who the customers are, and what they were looking for? Did he adequately assess the competition?

- Was the Metairie experience with pricing applicable to the Covington analysis? Would you expect the margin in Covington to be better or worse?

- Would it have been more prudent to start selling to the area from Metairie, watching its progress, and opening a branch a year later? Was the "window of opportunity" likely to close before then?

- What are the longer-term consequences of becoming a whole-sale/retail "hybrid?" Will this enhance or hinder the growth potential of the business? How will it affect the competitive situation? Are they entering a new business?

(2)   Acquire the most current and relevant data available

Start on the Internet, or at a good business library. Industry directories and periodicals, the more recent the better, can give useful statistics, analyze trends, and provide projections. Trade associations and vendors can frequently provide data specific to the business you plan to enter. Universities, government offices, and chambers of commerce can frequently help with location-specific information. Census data is frequently rich in the kinds of information we need. Computer searches on key words relating to our market can yield numerous valuable reference articles.

It is often difficult to convince prospective entrepreneurs to do a thorough job of market research. They are often unaware of how useful the information available can be, and of its relevance to their specific project.

For example: Interested in opening a golf equipment store? There are 25 million golfers in the U.S.; 7 million of them play at least 25 times per year. A recent survey of business executives showed that 61% of men and 33% of women have either called in sick or left work early to play golf.

What does this have to do with the business of our choice? Directly, it shows market sizes and trends. Indirectly it can add to our level of sophistication about our industry, objectively confirm what we already knew, or challenge the assumptions on which we were going to base our plans.

Entrepreneurial Resources: Sample market research sources.

Start at the author's online library for a current and comprehensive list of links to sources of information. Useful print sources, particularly if you are looking at a retail venture, include:

- **Demographic picture of the area, and comparison to national norms:**

> *CACI Sourcebook of Demographics and Buying Power for Every County in the USA*
> *Age, Education, Employment; Housing Profile; Demographic Profile;*
> *Purchasing Potential Profile*
> *American Consumer Lists;*
> *"High-Potential Prospects with Incomes in Excess of $100,000"*
> *Counts and prospect list, by zip code*
> *U.S. Department of Commerce*
> *National data on a wide range of consumer products. industry prospects*

- **Economic and population projections for the area:**
> *State Planning Office, Department of Economic Development*
> *Economic Indicators, Population Projections*
> *University Business and Economic Research, Small Business Development Center*
> *Area Economic Development Foundations*
> *Area business publications*

- **More localized information**

> *Public records*
> *Sales tax collections, building permits, business incorporations*
> *Trade associations*
> *Real estate transfers, utility hookups*

Practical Activity: **Market Research, Used-Book Store**

Assume you are planning to open a store to sell used books.

- Identify the size of the industry and customer demographics.
- Search business directories for data on firms in the industry.
- Search databases and the Internet for relevant information.
- List all sources used, whether or not they proved productive.

(3)   Identify market segments

From our discussion of small business opportunities, we should have
an idea of the general product area in which our business will compete.
The next step is to clarify and refine the niche our business will fill,
and this process is driven by information gathered on the opportunity.

A basic decision to be made is where in the process of satisfying
consumer needs will our offering fall? The product delivery "chain"
may be thought of as consisting of:

- Product manufacture, characterized by large competitors, a
  large initial investment, and the need for an effective distribution system;

- Wholesaling, a function currently undergoing some consolida-
  tion, and requiring sources of supply, and a dealer network;

- Retailing, a highly competitive area with a number of specialty
  niches, and;

- Services, generally the easiest types of businesses to start, but
  the hardest to get to a high level of profitability.

Individual businesses are generally identified in one of these categories, even if operating in a manner that falls between two of them, or
that combines two or more.

Once the decision is made as to where in this spectrum our company
will operate, our idea can take on a little more "shape," and we can
begin the market research process. Frequently, the results of the
market research cause us to reevaluate where in the product delivery

process we will position our business (for discussion purposes, we will use the term product to include services).

Within the population of the prospective customers for our product (which could be a service), there are smaller groups, called market segments, with similar needs. Markets can be segmented along several different dimensions: product-related; geographic; "psychographic," or relating to traits, motives, and lifestyles; and demographic, relating to consumer age or income level.

Real Scenario 3: How many piano tuners can this place support?

A piano tuner recently moved to Buffalo, NY, and would like to assess the business possibilities for him in his new home. He plans to estimate how many piano tuners the greater Buffalo area can support, and compare that to the number listed in the phone book. How do we advise him as to how to estimate the "right" number of tuners for the area?

One approach is simply to guess. Would it be 1, 10, 50, or 100? Are you comfortable with this approach? I am not. An approach I would be comfortable with would be to search for data on estimates of how many piano tuners per capita there are in the U.S., and apply that ratio to the Buffalo area population (let's use 1.3 million). Is data on this likely to be available? Test your resourcefulness by trying to find it.

Assuming that data is not available, we must go to the "some assembly required" approach to estimating, that is, deriving the estimate from data which is available modified by related local and national data, norms, and "rules of thumb." While this seems so indirect as to be little better than just guessing, it can be a very useful exercise. If nothing else, it causes us to identify some important variables and how they relate to our business of interest. The inaccuracies of compounding estimates can be minimized by working in ranges to give us a "ballpark" figure.

How can I derive a meaningful estimate from generally available information? It would be interesting to know what percentage of American households own a piano, and how often they get it tuned. If the data is national, we may need to apply some local adjustment factor. Given the annual number of piano tunings, we can divide by the annual capacity of a tuner to determine how many are needed.

I will do an "off-the-top-of-my-head" calculation to illustrate the method, then leave it to you to provide real values:

Buffalo has about 400,000 households (population divided by 3 members average); 8% of American households own pianos. I can think of no reason to apply any local adjustment to this figure, so we are talking about roughly 32,000 pianos. My guess is that two-thirds of all pianos are merely furniture, so that the remainder of about 11,000 is played regularly and in need of tuning. Tuners recommend that a piano be serviced twice a year, but my guess is that the average is probably once a year for active pianos, or 11,000 tunings per year. A tuner can service 2 to 4 pianos a day; let us say 3 per day, 5 days a week, 50 weeks a year, or 750 tunings per year per tuner. To provide Buffalo's 11,000 annual tunings would require almost 15 tuners. The phone book lists 9. Sounds promising!

 **PUT YOURSELF IN THEIR SHOES**

- Is this a good approach? How many would you have guessed without this analysis? Does the result seem reasonable? Is this enough on which to base the opening of a business?

- Could it have been done more scientifically? How? Would discussions with piano tuners and music stores have been useful? Are there any journals worth consulting? Would a survey have helped?

- Are pianos in places other than homes? Are there tuners not listed in the yellow pages?

The Census of Retail Trade provides the average number of stores per capita for a variety of retail outlets. Based on their data, we can determine how well our proposed market area is served on a relative basis for the type of business we plan to start. For example, there is, on average, a stationery store for every 33,000 people; for every 26,000 people there is one bookstore and one nursery and garden supply store. The population can presumably support a barber shop for every 2,200 residents, and a furniture store for every 3,000.

The Marketing Plan

With the information gathered in the research phase, we can refine our business concept further by considering our "marketing mix," those decisions to be made for our marketing plan that are generally referred to as the "four P's:" We will take a first pass at the following decisions to continue our screening, then refine the answers for the business plan.

- **Product**

What is the product that the market needs? How well positioned are we to provide it? How will we differentiate ourselves from the competition?

What brand name and packaging will we use? How wide will our product line be? What will be its features, accessories and options?

- **Price**

Will our price be competition-based or quality-image-based? What is the range of pricing options? How price-sensitive are sales? Can we be low cost and high service?

What will our terms be? What discounts and allowances will we provide?

- **Promotion**

How will we promote the product? What aspects of the product should we stress? How and where will we advertise? What are the most cost-effective media? Can we afford an agency?

Are there some non-traditional promotional methods which could be effective? Does our venture lend itself to personal selling over mass-marketing, cross-promotions with related products? Are there opportunities for free publicity?

- **Place**

Where and how will we distribute the product? What will the distribution "channel" look like?

Real Scenario 4: Atlantic Brewing; Does anybody care how this stuff tastes?

Jim Patton and Rush Cumming met at the Boston Brew Club, found out that they lived near each other on the North shore, and began to carpool to meetings. Jim, a college professor, fancied himself quite the amateur brew master, and his home-brewed beers frequently won taste contests at the Club. Rush, a self-employed carpenter, was more interested in the tastings than the recipes, but enjoyed the conversations with Jim about the fine art of small-batch brewing.

It was an article of faith among members of such clubs, all over the country, that the products of the large commercial breweries were bland so as not to offend any of their mass clientele; greater emphasis was thought to be placed on shelf-life than on taste. By the mid-1980s, Jim and Rush were tracking with great interest the beginning of a new industry, the "microbrewery," where the techniques of home brewing were adapted to a minimal commercial scale.

Jim visited a microbrewery in Pennsylvania, meeting the designer and builder of their equipment, an Englishman named Fred Glick, who had become something of a cult figure in the industry. Fred responded to Jim's interest in starting a microbrewery by roughing out a design that would meet Jim's specifications, and an estimate of the cost of building the state-of-the-art equipment.

On the flight home, Jim developed the outline of a business plan, and a rather detailed estimate of startup funds required. The funds were well beyond his means, but he and Rush could provide the seed money to prepare a private placement stock offering and present their story to prospective investors. Jim had already picked out the location of the microbrewery, near his home in Peabody, and a company name, The Atlantic Brewing Company.

The product was clear in his mind, a beer free of preservatives and made with a locally available spring water. They would produce a lighter brew, "Golden," and a heartier "Amber." Seasonal and specialty beers would also be made as production schedules allowed. Their products would be priced with imported beers, while offering greater quality and freshness. They would appeal to all premium beer drinkers, not just the connoisseurs.

Since the cost of bottling equipment was prohibitive, they would begin by distributing kegs only. This would require competing for tap space at bars and restaurants, initially on the Northshore with its affluent demographic, while attempting to develop a following in Boston area bars with college-student clienteles. They would distribute directly, delivering in company trucks.

Now all they needed were a few investors...

 **PUT YOURSELF IN THEIR SHOES**

- How would you rate the marketing plan? How is Atlantic differentiated from the competition? What need are they filling? Are we convinced that need exists?
- Analyze their pricing strategy. What is their greatest competition?
- Suggest a marketing campaign that emphasizes Atlantic's strengths. To whom are they trying to appeal? What is the best way to reach them?

Breakeven Analysis

With a marketing mix determined, we can take our first look at the financial prospects for the venture. While many people are uncomfortable with the "guesswork" involved in projecting sales and expenses for a prospective business, there are approaches which at least yield structured guesswork, similar to the marketing research estimates earlier. In any case of predicting future events, there is no right answer, and if we are careful our judgment is as good as anyone's on our own business concept.

Breakeven analysis is a good way to develop a sense of the feasibility of a venture. It is a way to determine what level of sales is required to allow the venture to generate just enough "margin dollars" to cover its expenses. Margin is the amount of money left over after the cost of the goods sold is deducted. The process is best understood by example, and a continuation of the Southland Plumbing Supply case will be used:

Real Scenario 5: How much do we have to sell to make it there?

In February of 1977, John Vinturella of Southland Plumbing Supply was "commissioned" to open a branch of the Metairie, LA company in Covington, LA, 40 miles to the north. A marketing plan was devised, and the next step was to determine whether the expected sales level of the branch would support profitable operation.

From parish permit information, John estimated the amount of money to be spent on homebuilding and remodeling over the next year. Information from the Bureau of Labor Statistics allowed him to determine the percentage of that amount to be spent on plumbing materials. BLS data also provided an estimate of repair and replacement expenditures for existing homes.

After estimating the total amount of plumbing material sales in the market area, and analyzing the competitive situation, he assumed a

75% market share for the new branch (sound reasonable?). This yielded an expected sales figure, and from the ranges in his calculations, he decided on pessimistic and optimistic values for monthly sales (see following table).

EXPENSES			BREAKEVEN ANALYSIS		
Salaries	John	$2,000	*Expenses*	$8,000	per month
	Others	$2,000			
	Benefits (25%)	$1,000	From Metairie Experience:		
Equipment	Trucks	$300	*Margin*	20%	per sales $
Leases	Other	$60			
Expenses	Transportation	$430	*Sales needed to generate expense $:*		
	Insurance	$360		Exp/Mar	$40,000
	Legal/Acctg	$150			
	Utilities	$300	*Estimated sales*		
	Supplies	$420		Low	$35,000
	Advertising	$100		Expected	$45,000
	Miscellaneous	$100		High	$60,000
Contingency	(10%)	$727			
TOTAL		$7,997			

To generate this monthly statement, John estimated that he would need two other people to adequately run the branch, a warehouseman and a delivery person. A delivery truck would be needed, and his new "car" would be a small pickup truck; these would be leased. Furniture requirements would be minimal, and shelving for inventory could be built inexpensively.

Total expenses to operate the branch would be on the order of $8,000 per month. These are all essentially fixed costs, that is they are relatively constant within the estimated range of sales volume. Variable, or sales-volume-dependent, costs consist of only the cost of goods sold, estimated to be 80% of sales, based on the experience in Metairie.

The level of sales required to break even, then, is that sales volume at which the remaining 20% of revenues (margin) generates enough gross profit to pay expenses. In this case that number is $8,000/20%, or $40,000. This is below the estimate of the most likely sales volume, so there is a reasonable expectation of this being a profitable venture.

TIME OUT! - YOUR COACH SAYS

1. How would you rate the quality of the market research used to justify this venture? What would you have done differently / in addition?

2. Given the information used in John's analysis, would you have opened the branch? Are they trying to justify opening the branch irrespective of what the data shows?

3. Where John's expense estimates to vague? How could they have been refined? Were the expense categories reasonable and complete? Is the market share estimate realistic?

Lets review the components of breakeven analysis in more general terms:

(1)   Estimate monthly sales

If possible, it is better to "derive" a sales estimate than simply to pick one. For example, we may first try to find an estimate of the total demand for our product in our market area; market research will often yield a fairly well founded number for this, or provide norms, which can be used.

Next an estimate of what share of that demand our company might reasonably be expected to capture can be multiplied by total demand to give the sales estimate. It is often useful to establish a sales range, for example, pessimistic, likely, and optimistic sales levels.

(2)   Estimate monthly expenses

Identify the major expense categories for operating the business; SBA publishes a "Checklist for Going Into Business," which contains some helpful worksheets. Make estimates of how much you would spend in each of those categories each month. Distinguish fixed costs from variable costs which depend on level of sales. Figure a total of monthly expenses. Estimate always on the conservative side. The natural tendency is to "cut too close" on expense figures, and the less visible costs such as permits and taxes are frequently overlooked. The above example missed one fairly basic expense. Have you figured which? How much should it have been? (Remember that these are 1977 dollars).

Note also in the example that 25% is added to the payroll figure for benefits. This might cover federal and state taxes, unemployment insurance, and sick and vacation time, but little else. If you plan to contribute to hospitalization insurance or educational costs, or other benefits, this figure should be increased accordingly.

The example also includes a figure for "Miscellaneous" expenses, and an added "Contingency" of 10% of total expenses. Is this enough to account for the omission?

(3)   Calculate breakeven sales level

Determine your margin. For example, if you buy your product for $0.80 and sell it for $1, then $0.20 or 20% of each sales dollar is margin with which to pay expenses. If expenses are $8,000 per month, sales of $40,000 (20% of $40,000 is $8,000) represents a break even situation.

Many businesses deal in markup rather than margin. For example, if I buy a product for $0.80 and sell it for $1, I have marked it up $0.20, or 25% of my cost of goods. To minimize confusion, we will deal in margin rather than markup percentages.

(4)   Compare and conclude

Where in our range of estimates does the breakeven sales figure fall? If it is above our optimistic estimate, prospects are grim. If it is around our expected figure, we may need to look a bit more closely. If it indicates that we can break even with a sales figure below our pessimistic estimate, or comfortably below our expected sales, it makes the cut.

Breakeven analysis is only a screening device, to help us sort out promising ventures from hopeless causes. We will discuss "serious" financial planning later, after we have chosen a prospective business for detailed analysis.

Once an opportunity passes the "screen test," we must then evaluate whether there might be an alternative to starting a new business. In some product areas, the chances for success are enhanced by acquiring a franchise. In some cases, purchase of an existing business can avoid the start-up trauma, while eliminating a competitor.

Summary

Once a business idea is determined to be worthy of further consideration, we must assess its potential in detail. This is often an iterative process; as we select an approach to the market and do the necessary research, we may detect greater potential in a different approach and have to revise and repeat the research process.

The first basic decision to be made is where in the product delivery chain do we position ourselves. If there is a service that we expect to expand rapidly, we may choose to provide that service, or to supply some of the required materials to those who provide it, or even to manufacture some of the required materials.

With this decision made, subject to being revisited, we can design a research effort to assess the potential of this approach to the market. The first step is to determine what we need to know, that is what available information is the most meaningful in the measurement of the opportunity.

Again the decisions are rather basic. What market will we serve? Who are our customers? What are they looking for? What is the competitive situation?

Effective Internet "surfing," or visiting a business library can be good starting points. We can start with a "reconnaissance mission" to determine how much of what we would like to know is readily available. Often our market research objectives must be modified to use available information. In some cases, we may choose to survey the market to acquire data designed specifically to our needs. In every case, we must apply some judgment to the data, since we are trying to project our future prospects.

From the marketing research results, we must refine our marketing plan. What will our product be? What is our competitive advantage or distinctive competence? How will we price the product? How will we promote it? How will we distribute it?

TIME OUT! - YOUR COACH SAYS

1. Who are the most likely customers for the opportunities we discussed, i.e. the coffee shop and used-book store? What are they buying? Are their price expectations realistic?

2. What would a good market research strategy be for each of these ven-tures? What would it be for a venture you may be considering?

Chapter 4
The "Compleat" Entrepreneur

From World Wide Words:

[Q] "Are compleat and complete really two separate words, as the American Heritage Dictionary seems to say? While compleat is said to mean 'quintessential', one meaning of complete is closely related as 'skilled; accomplished'."

[A] In Britain, compleat is archaic, used in writing only as a bit of whimsy, and at that rather rarely. It is more common in North America, though often equally whimsical; a quick search of the Web turned up more than 40,000 instances, of which all those I sampled were from the USA.

The Oxford English Dictionary says that one sense of the word (in either spelling) is the one you quoted—referring to a person who is accomplished, "especially in reference to a particular art or pursuit".

This sense was reintroduced in the archaic spelling at the beginning of the twentieth century by Isaak Walton, the author of The Compleat Angler, or the Contemplative Man's Recreation; Being a Discourse of Fish and Fishing, not unworthy the perusal of most Anglers. Writing in 1653, he naturally used the older spelling of complete and modern editions retain it.

<u>Home-Based Business</u>

You wake up to an inbox full of email. An overnight package is delivered. It's business as usual; just another day at the office. However, unlike most traditional offices in the country, there's a baby sleeping in the next room, a dog playing out back, and the smell of a homemade breakfast wafting through the air. This is the new work-place of the 2000s - the Home Office.

What's behind the move to the Home Office? Modern technology. Powerful computers, high-speed Internet connections, laser and color printers, cellular phones, and toll free phone numbers are now easily accessible and affordable to home based businesses. The Wall Street Journal recently reported that "...most home based businesses especially startups can stick to the basics and equip themselves for $3,000 to $5,000."

There are many advantages to working from home; no commuting time, flexible hours, casual dress, proximity to children and the "comforts" of home. "Clearly, the home-office is the wave of the future and is here to stay," says Richard Ekstract, chairman of the Home Office Association of America (HOAA). "Where else could you become a great success in your field and still be able to send the kids off to school and welcome them in the afternoon when they come home?"

According to IDC, a top national research firm, there are between 34.3 million and 36.6 million home office households in the United States alone. They also conducted a recent survey indicating that the average income for income-generating home office households is $63,000 a year.

The SBA's Office of Advocacy reports that in 2000 nearly 20,000 entrepreneurs grossed more than $1 million operating from a home-based environment. Estimates are that the share of households in the United States involved in home-based businesses is approaching 50%.

And these businesses enjoy a healthy rate of success. About 70% of home-based businesses will last over a three-year period, compared to 29% of other business ventures, according to the Home-Based Business Institute. Find/SVP reports that 89% with household incomes greater than $80,000 have a home office compared to 14% of those with incomes below $25,000.

According to the Small Business Administration, today more than half (53%) of the small businesses in the U.S. are home-based. Entrepreneur magazine estimates that $427 billion is generated each year by home-based businesses. That is bigger than General Motors, Ford, and Chrysler combined. According to IDC, home-based businesses create an estimated 8,500 new jobs daily.

So, it's pretty much can't-miss? Not so fast. The Federal Trade Commission, www.ftc.gov, suggests you be on your guard when you see an ad promising:

- *Be part of one of America's Fastest Growing Industries!*
- *Earn thousand of dollars a month - from your home - Processing Medical Billing Claims.*

You can find ads like this everywhere - from the street light and telephone pole on your corner to your newspaper and PC. While you may find these ads appealing, especially if you can't work outside your home, proceed with caution. Not all work-at-home opportunities deliver on their promises.

Many ads omit the fact that you may have to work many hours without pay. Or they don't disclose all the costs you will have to pay. Countless work-at-home schemes require you to spend your own money to place newspaper ads; make photocopies; or buy the envelopes, paper, stamps, and other supplies or equipment you need to do the job. The companies sponsoring the ads also may demand that you pay for instructions or "tutorial" software. Consumers deceived by these ads have lost thousands of dollars, in addition to their time and energy.

Several types of offers are classic work-at-home schemes.

Medical billing

Ads for pre-packaged businesses - known as billing centers - are in newspapers, on television and on the Internet. If you respond, you'll get a sales pitch that may sound like this: There's "a crisis" in the health care system, due partly to the overwhelming task of processing paper claims. The solution is electronic claim processing. Because only a small percentage of claims are transmitted electronically, the market for billing centers is wide open.

The promoter also may tell you that many doctors who process claims electronically want to "outsource" or contract out their billing services to save money. Promoters will promise that you can earn a substantial income working full or part time, providing services like billing, accounts receivable, electronic insurance claim processing and practice management to doctors and dentists. They also may assure you that no experience is required, that they will provide clients eager to buy your services or that their qualified salespeople will find clients for you.

The reality: you will have to sell. These promoters rarely provide experienced sales staff or contacts within the medical community.

The promoter will follow up by sending you materials that typically include a brochure, application, sample diskettes, a contract (licensing agreement), disclosure document, and in some cases, testimonial letters, videocassettes and reference lists. For your investment of $2,000 to $8,000, a promoter will promise software, training and technical support. And the company will encourage you to call its references.

Make sure you get many names from which to choose. If only one or two names are given, they may be "shills" - people hired to give favorable testimonials. It's best to interview people in person, prefera-bly where the business operates, to reduce your risk of being misled by shills and also to get a better sense of how the business works.

Few consumers who purchase a medical billing business opportunity are able to find clients, start a business and generate revenues - let alone recover their investment and earn a substantial income. Competition in the medical billing market is fierce and revolves around a number of large and well-established firms.

Envelope stuffing

Promoters usually advertise that, for a "small" fee, they will tell you how to earn money stuffing envelopes at home. Later - when it's too late - you find out that the promoter never had any employment to offer. Instead, for your fee, you're likely to get a letter telling you to place the same "envelope-stuffing" ad in newspapers or magazines, or to send the ad to friends and relatives. The only way you'll earn money is if people respond to your work-at-home ad.

Assembly or craft work

These programs often require you to invest hundreds of dollars in equipment or supplies. Or they require you to spend many hours producing goods for a company that has promised to buy them. For example, you might have to buy a sewing or sign-making machine from the company, or materials to make items like aprons, baby shoes or plastic signs.

However, after you've purchased the supplies or equipment and performed the work, fraudulent operators don't pay you. In fact, many consumers have had companies refuse to pay for their work because it didn't meet "quality standards."

Unfortunately, no work is ever "up to standard," leaving workers with relatively expensive equipment and supplies - and no income. To sell their goods, these workers must find their own customers.

Questions to Ask

Legitimate work-at-home program sponsors should tell you - in writing - what's involved in the program they are selling. Here are some questions you might ask a promoter:

- What tasks will I have to perform? (Ask the program sponsor to list every step of the job.)
- Will I be paid a salary or will my pay be based on commission?

- Who will pay me?
- When will I get my first paycheck?
- What is the total cost of the work-at-home program, including supplies, equipment and membership fees? What will I get for my money?

The answers to these questions may help you determine whether a work-at-home program is appropriate for your circumstances, and whether it is legitimate.

You also might want to check out the company with your local consumer protection agency, state Attorney General and the Better Business Bureau, not only where the company is located, but also where you live. These organizations can tell you whether they have received complaints about the work-at-home program that interests you. But be wary: the absence of complaints doesn't necessarily mean the company is legitimate. Unscrupulous companies may settle complaints, change their names or move to avoid detection.

Where to Complain

If you have spent money and time on a work-at-home program and now believe the program may not be legitimate, contact the company and ask for a refund. Let company representatives know that you plan to notify officials about your experience. If you can't resolve the dispute with the company, file a complaint with these organizations:

- The Attorney General's office in your state or the state where the company is located. The office will be able to tell you whether you're protected by any state law that may regulate work-at-home programs.
- Your local consumer protection offices.
- Your local Better Business Bureau.
- Your local postmaster. The U.S. Postal Service investigates fraudulent mail practices.
- The advertising manager of the publication that ran the ad. The manager may be interested to learn about the problems you've had with the company.

Franchising

A franchise is a continuing relationship between a franchisor and a franchisee in which the franchisor's knowledge, image, success, manufacturing, and marketing techniques are supplied to the franchisee for a consideration. This consideration usually consists of a high "up-front" fee, and a significant royalty percentage, which generally require a fairly long time to recover.

About 10% of the 20 million U.S. businesses operate under some kind of franchise agreement. About 3,000 companies sell franchises to on the order of 25,000 new buyers each year, or about one every 20 minutes.

Franchises account for over a third of all retail sales. Franchising offers those who lack business experience (but do not lack capital) a business with a good probability of success. It is a ready-made business, with all the incentives of a small business combined with the management skills of a large one. It is a way to be "in business for yourself, not by yourself."

Franchises take many forms. Some are simply trade-name licensing arrangements, such as TrueValue Hardware, where the franchisee is provided product access and participation in an advertising cooperative. Some trade name licenses, particularly in skin-care products, are part of a multi-level marketing system, where a franchisee can designate sub-franchisees and benefit from their efforts.

Others might be distributorships, or manufacturer's representative arrangements, such as automobile dealerships, or gasoline stations. It could be Jane's Cadillac, or Fred's Texaco; the product is supplied by the franchisor, but the franchisee has a fair amount of latitude in how the business is located, designed and run. The franchisor will frequently specify showroom requirements and inventory level criteria, and could grant either exclusive or non-exclusive franchise areas.

The most familiar type of franchise, however, is probably the "total concept" store such as McDonald's. Pay your franchise fee, and they will "roll out" a store for you to operate.

The advantages can be considerable. The franchise fee buys instant product recognition built and maintained by sophisticated advertising and marketing programs. The franchisor's management experience and depth assists the franchisee by providing employee guidelines, policies and procedures, operating experience, and sometimes even financial assistance. They provide proven methods for determining promising locations, and a successful store design and equipment configuration. Centralized purchasing gives large-buyer "clout" to each location.

The large initial cost can be difficult to raise. The highly structured environment can be more limiting than it is reassuring. Continuing royalty costs take a significant portion of profits. Several small business periodicals evaluate and rank franchise opportunities. There are now several franchise "matchmaking" firms who can assist in the evaluation process.

Is the franchisor professional? Evaluate them on the clarity of the agreement, and how well your rights are protected, the strength of their training and support program, and their commitment to your success. Be sure to talk to current franchisees about their experiences. Beware of a franchisor committed to a rate of growth that exceeds their ability to manage; they may not be sufficiently interested in the sales they have already made.

Real Scenario 6:   SpeeDee Oil Change of St. Charles Ave.

Gary Copp and Kevin Bennett met at Loyola University in the early 1970s as each pursued a business degree and considered future prospects. Both wanted to start a business at some point in the near future, and they kept in touch as each took a sales job on graduation.

Many of their get-togethers were spent brainstorming about business possibilities. Staying close to their personal interests, many of the opportunities they discussed related to automobiles or sports. As their ideas began to become more tangible with time, their attention was focusing more and more on servicing cars.

Kevin's uncle owned a service station on a busy corner in Metairie LA (suburban New Orleans), and had a little extra space to one side that was offered to them for a related use. It was decided to start a car wash as a "pilot project" in a sense for what they might want to do ultimately. G&K Enterprises was formed to operate the car wash, and employees were hired so that Gary and Kevin could keep their "day jobs." A considerable amount of time was spent by both at the car wash, supervising, doing bookkeeping work, and watching and listening.

Though this venture consumed most of their spare time, they knew they were on the right track. At the same time, the "service" in auto service stations was undergoing a dramatic transformation; many stations were converting a gasoline island, or the entire station, to self-service. Few stations had attendants to check under the hood and tell you when your oil was dirty, or remind you that it was time for some regular or seasonal service. Automobile warranties were getting longer, but requiring documentation that maintenance services were performed at prescribed intervals.

A market need had been created and, at the time, there was only one company with national aspirations performing the services that the gasoline stations had abandoned. Jiffy Lube had begun in the northeast U.S. and was setting the standard for the industry that G&K would enter. Jiffy's offered these services with the added benefit of a 10-minute guarantee for an oil change, lubrication, and maintenance check. Based on owner's manual specifications, they would remind you of service intervals and requirements, and suggest other indicated maintenance procedures.

G&K sensed that it was still early enough for them to seize a leadership position in the industry. They converted their car wash into a quick oil change facility. A rolling oil can logo was developed and the name "SpeeDee" was chosen. Kevin still jokes that their 9-minute guarantee was not to one-up Jiffy, but to save SpeeDee money on a sign that was priced by the letter.

Their prototype was an instant success, and by the time they had opened three more outlets in the New Orleans area they realized they had a winner. Their profits allowed them to become full-time employees of the venture, and to package the SpeeDee Oil Change System (SOCS) for franchising.

GROWING PAINS

The company began to sell regional rights to sub-franchisors around the U.S. while maintaining the Gulf South region for themselves. Regions were tailored to the interests of prospective investors; early regions included New England, East Texas, and greater Los Angeles. Regional owners would then open stores or license franchisees throughout their franchise areas. These would all be new locations built to national specifications, unlike Jiffy's approach to achieve rapid growth by acquiring existing independents.

The SOCS strategy was to create a strong additional layer of co-entrepreneurs, the region owners, to become a national company in a short amount of time. By the late 1980s this strategy was beginning to take hold, but the cash demands on SOCS exceeded their expectations. They decided that they needed to direct more of their attention to developing their own region, the Gulf Coast, to improve their cash flow before returning to their national roll-out.

SPEEDEE ON THE AVENUE

There was one location in New Orleans that Kevin had always coveted for a SpeeDee outlet, St. Charles Avenue. To locals it is reverently referred to as "The Avenue;" a ride on the St. Charles streetcar is a recommended tourist attraction. In 1988, a location became available with the planned demolition of a seedy convenience store.

Unable to finance a company-owned shop at the site, Kevin offered a franchise on the property to a "drinking buddy," Al Serio. Al ran a very successful hardware store with his younger brother George, and was sufficiently well-heeled to finance the deal. Al asked Kevin for some time to discuss it with George and with their older brother Jerry, a successful computer consultant.

Al was not a very effective salesman in the meeting with his brothers. He could only do it if they joined him; he did not have the time or that much interest, but he felt obliged to Kevin. Jerry, whose schedule was a bit more flexible, said he would help if the others were interested, but it would not be his choice. George surprised his brothers by saying that he was a bit frustrated at being second-in-command at the hardware store, and that this might give him the opportunity to show his talents by being in charge of something.

George's comments turned the tide, changing the conversation from why they should not purchase the franchise to discussing the details of how they would run it. Al suggested a good candidate for shop manager under George's supervision. Jerry remembered an old friend in the auto parts business who could supply them and help with inventory control.

Al found out from his banker that their strong financial position would allow them to "borrow out," or finance the project entirely with debt. They would lease the land for $2,500 per month, borrow $200,000 secured by the building and equipment, and get a $100,000 credit line for franchise and start-up fees, and for working capital.

DECISION TIME

Kevin provided the Serios with some rather detailed expense information on the operation of a franchise. Jerry then factored in the financing details and developed pro-forma income statements for scenarios representing break-even, and expected and optimistic situations suggested by Kevin (see Attachment).

The general practice in the industry was to close only on Sundays; estimates were based on 26 sales days per month. Many outlets did as much business on Saturdays as on two weekdays.

The key income variables in the operation of the franchise are the number of cars serviced per day (called "rolls"), and the average invoice amount. The oil change is basically a break-even proposition generating about a $25 ticket. To succeed, an operator has to generate enough add-on sales, such as tune-ups and radiator flushes, to double the average ticket.

The key expense variable is payroll cost, viewed as a percent of sales. This is controlled not by paying low salaries, but by keeping the shop busy, thereby spreading a basically fixed cost over a larger sales figure. The more successful outlets kept their payroll costs on the order of 20%.

The traffic-count for the location was excellent, about 50% higher than what was considered the threshold for a SpeeDee outlet; this suggested that they should have little trouble meeting a target of 40 rolls per day. The location is in the commuting pattern for the prosperous uptown part of the city, about three-quarters of the way downtown. The surroundings were a moderately busy commercial area on St. Charles, with generally low-income housing off the Avenue.

PUT YOURSELF IN THEIR SHOES

- Can Jerry's Quick Oil Change compete with SpeeDee?
- Does the franchise deliver business that we might not have gotten anyway?

TIME OUT! – YOUR COACH SAYS:
You may want to consider:

1. Are the vision and values of this firm aligned with your own? Even if you hire someone else to manage the business, expect to spend allot of time with the operation.

2. Is the name well known? If not, what are you paying for? Is the fee structure reasonable and are all costs clearly described?

SpeeDee Oil Change	ST. CHARLES AVENUE			
	Days	26	26	26
	Cars/Day	36	40	45
	Avg Invoice	$41.82	$50.00	$52.00
		BrkEven	Expected	Optimistic
Net Sales		$39,144	$52,000	$60,840
Cost of Sales	25.0%	$9,786	$13,000	$15,210
GROSS MARGIN		$29,358	$39,000	$45,630
		=====	=====	======
Payroll w/Taxes (% of Sales)		26.6%	22.0%	19.0%
		$10,425	$11,440	$11,560
Occupancy (Land/Bldg/Tax)		$5,075	$5,075	$5,075
Franchise Costs		$5,872	$7,800	$9,126
Advertising	10.0%	$3,914	$5,200	$6,084
Royalties	5.0%	$1,957	$2,600	$3,042
Insurance		$1,156	$1,220	$1,264
Garage/General/Wk Comp		$960	$960	$960
Damage Claims	0.5%	$196	$260	$304
Services		$2,052	$2,168	$2,248
Bank, Misc. Fees		$700	$700	$700
CredCd Discount	0.9%	$352	$468	$548
Shop Services		$1,000	$1,000	$1,000
Office Expense		$955	$955	$955
Shop Expense		$900	$900	$900
Debt Service		$2,923	$2,923	$2,923
TOTAL EXPENSES		$29,358	$32,481	$34,050
PROFIT/LOSS		$0	$6,519	$11,580

While franchising is often billed as a safe path to riches, an increasingly vocal group of critics, including several franchisee associations, are warning prospective franchisees to beware. "The problem isn't that franchising is a bad concept," said Robert Purvin, chairman of the American Association of Franchisees and Dealers. "It's that franchising has become such a seller's market that many people are buying into bad systems."

Buying an Existing Business

If a franchise for our chosen opportunity is not feasible, our other alternative to starting a business is to buy an existing business. To some extent, buying a business is less risky because its operating history provides meaningful data on its chances of success under our concept. We must, however, balance the acquisition cost against what the cost of a startup might have been.

One important factor is the seller's reasons for offering the business for sale. Often these are for personal and career reasons, such as a readiness to retire with the absence of a successor, or another opportunity perceived as a better fit. Where there are business reasons for selling, such as personnel problems, or inability to stand up to the competition, we must decide whether all that is missing is a quality of management that we can provide, or that there are some changes we can make in the way the business is operated that will make the difference.

Due diligence must be performed before a binding offer is made. Is the company's history and network of business relationships clear? Are their financial statements representative? What do they say about the business? Are there any unstated dangers or risks? Are there any hidden liabilities? Often, a review of the financials by our banker and accountant can be valuable.

How "good" an organization is it? How is it perceived by its customers and suppliers? If we do not buy it, how tough a competitor will it be? What will be the effect of an ownership change on the customer base, supplier relations, etc.? How much customer loyalty is to the business, and how much to the current owner?

Does the company have a "niche?" Is it the one in which you want to operate? Is there a competitive advantage to the operation that is sustainable? Are its assets useful to you? Will key personnel remain with the business?

If the decision is made that purchase of an existing business could improve our chances for success, we must then evaluate existing businesses to determine whether any are available at a price that is economically more favorable than a new venture. How do we value a business?

Before examining specific techniques for business evaluation, it must be emphasized that there is no one correct value for a business. Any valuation is based on assumptions, and projections of future performance. As in our breakeven analysis discussion, discomfort about basing financial decisions on assumptions and projections are natural.

Entrepreneurship requires exploring uncharted territory, and operating in an environment of uncertainty. Success depends on applying our best judgment to reducing that uncertainty.

Real Scenario 7:   Are personal computers just a passing fad?

When Clay Olson opened a retail computer store in Charlotte, NC, in 1983, he was a bit ahead of his time. All he could sell were Commodore VIC-20s and Atari computers that he purchased from an appliance wholesaler, and the public was not yet convinced of their utility. His furniture business could absorb the losses incurred then, but this time he would do it differently. His retail computer store now, in 1988, would be a separate company, well-staffed, and well stocked with the best lines; the industry had matured so much that even IBM, his former employer, had entered.

His inclination was to buy an existing store, and one day an ad in the newspaper's "Business-to-Business" listings caught his eye. A small computer retailer/assembler was listed by a local business broker. Clay read the package given him by the broker, and requested a meeting with the owner.

Clay found the owner, Sam Romer, difficult to read. Sam was an interesting character, 30-ish with a hint of a foreign accent and a "know-it-all" demeanor. By his account, he had the buying connections to purchase high-quality components from little-known manufacturers, and that he and his technician would then assemble and fine-tune them. Their competitive advantage was then that they could sell high-performance computers for the price of "off-the-shelf mediocrities."

The customer list, oriented toward university and government users, was very impressive. There was no established marketing program, and little company recognition outside the customer list. Many of their sales were attained by competitive bid, generally several units at a time with small profit margins. Financial records were very disorganized, and Clay noticed that the company, which had earlier been incorporated as ByteWyse, Inc., had recently been converted into a proprietorship.

Sam seemed to have a good grasp of the technical aspects of the business, and a confidence-building if not completely likeable sales manner. He offered as his reason for selling that he wanted to return to graduate school, and that he could continue to sell for the buyers on a commission basis. If Clay chose not to use him, Sam would sign a one-year non-compete agreement. The technician, a real "hacker," was willing to stay on to do purchasing and system assembly for the new owners.

The sale price was $75,000; Sam valued the equipment and inventory at about two-thirds of that.

The equipment seemed to be current and well-kept, and the inventory was well organized. Clay would then be paying about $25,000 for the customer list and purchasing relationships. He asked Sam for about a week to think about it before returning for further discussion.

PUT YOURSELF IN THEIR SHOES

- Does Clay have enough information to make an offer? What else should he do? Is there any one with whom he should consult for advice?

- How do you feel about the "intangibles?" Are you satisfied with Sam's reasons for selling the business? How do you feel about keeping him on as a salesman?

- What exactly is Clay buying? Is he likely to retain existing customers? Could he not establish similar buying relationships anyway? Should he keep the technician?

- Does the company give Clay a "running start" in the business? Does it offer a better foundation for growth than a start-up? Is it limiting in any way?

- Should Clay make a lower offer? Based on what? For how much? What should his negotiating strategy be?

Business Valuation

Small-business sales are generally (on the order of 94%) sales of assets, with no assumption of liabilities; the remainder are sales of company stock. Often the seller finances part of the purchase; typically the buyer makes a down payment on the order of one-third of the sales price, with repayment terms of five years at market rates. Do you see any danger for the seller in financing the sale?

The most difficult issue in small business sales is establishing a selling price. It is an inexact science, characterized by a seller's too-high expectations, and an overly skeptical prospective buyer.

We will consider three basic methods of evaluating a business: a market approach; a book-value approach; and, an earnings approach.

The market approach is the simplest method, basing the value of the business on projections of earnings multiplied by a typical price/earnings ratio for the industry. While this technique applies to transactions involving publicly-traded companies, it is seldom applicable to the small closely-held company. There is a ready market for a few shares of a public company, but small businesses are not so easy to "turn-over," and their generally local nature makes them more vulnerable to economic cycles. Financial practices and reporting are also generally less consistent in smaller businesses than in the larger ones on which most industry-wide averages are based.

These inconsistencies cause most business valuators to "re-cast" the financial statements of closely-held companies. For many of these firms, earnings are understated; whereas larger firms try to maximize profits, the objective of most smaller firms is to minimize taxes. How is this strategy implemented? While the vast majority of small businesses use aggressive but clearly ethical methods, opportunities exist for abuse.

Owners can manipulate family member salaries based on the relative advantages of paying personal versus corporate taxes. They can pay family members who do not really work there. Personal expenses could be charged to a company account. Assets could be understated, and/or liabilities overstated. In businesses which make a lot of cash sales, some could be made without invoices, with the owner "pocketing" the proceeds. Are these practices illegal? Are they unethical?

We will now outline the more commonly applied methods of valuation, then illustrate them with a case study.

(1)   Earnings

The earnings approach to valuing a business views the business as one more option for investing our money, that is, given our assessment of the risk involved, we have a certain expectation of return. We would certainly expect a greater return than on securities backed by the U.S. Treasury, but would possibly accept a lesser return than on a highly speculative venture.

Let us say that we have an opportunity to buy a business for $240,000 that projects annual earnings of a little over $40,000. This is an annual return on investment of about 18%, based on the owner's projections. Let us say further that it is a stable, mature business with a clear financial history and relatively little risk. Is 18% return satisfactory? It depends largely on the quality of the projections, and alternative investment possibilities.

Is the owner's projection likely to be objective? What are alternative methods of projecting earnings? Are economic conditions consistent enough for a historical average to be meaningful?

Are there any "dark clouds on the horizon" for the market area, or for the industry? What is the competitive situation? How is the business' market share? What are the long-term prospects for a small independent company in this industry?

Are last year's earnings a good indicator of earnings for the next few years? Were there any unusual circumstances? Are they likely to be repeated? Can we make a better estimate? What will we base it on? What is the quality of the financial records? Are there useful trade sources?

Could earnings be improved when we take over? Do we see waste, overpayment for materials or services, excess or excessively paid employees? How does the owner's pay and perquisites compare to our "opportunity cost," that is, the amount we could earn elsewhere?

Could earnings not be as good as they seem? Is equipment in disrepair or space insufficient? Will key employees leave the company? Will they be committed to a new owner? Will a major customer be lost? Are key buying relationships assured? Is company reputation an asset or liability?

Are there better investments available, without the everyday worries of business ownership? Do we prefer the business owner lifestyle to passive investment?

(2)   Book Value

The book-value of a corporation is generally shown on its balance sheet as "Net Worth," or "Owner's Equity." It represents the excess value of the company's assets over its liabilities. What is implied in accepting this value as a sales price? It assumes that all components of the balance sheet are fairly valued, and that the assets are useful to the new owner's mission. Book-value sales are almost always based on adjustments to the balance sheet. What do we look at more closely?

Balance sheet items that are generally deserving of closer inspection include:

CURRENT ASSETS
- Accounts Receivable: How current are they? Discount by age.
- Notes Receivable: How collectable are they? What are the payment terms?
- Inventory: Is it counted correctly? How is it costed? Is allowance made for overstock and obsolete items?

LONG-TERM ASSETS
- Depreciation is a tax device, applied as aggressively as the law allows.
- Assets should be revalued in their current state, by market or replacement value.
- The seller may want to keep, and the buyer not want to buy, some assets.

How do we verify the adjustments? We may need to take inventory ourselves, and to have professional appraisals of the physical assets. This is not to say that the conscientious buyer cannot sometimes still be misled.

Other variations on the process might be where the buyer would pay adjusted book value plus 2 or 3 years earnings, or might buy only selected assets. Frequently the selling price can vary depending on the terms, such as the amount of seller financing, years to repay, and interest rate.

As an example of this evaluation process, let us take another look at the Covington, LA plumbing wholesale operation:

Real Scenario 8:   Tammany Supply, Inc. (A)

In February of 1977, John Vinturella of Southland Plumbing Supply was "commissioned" to open a branch of the Metairie, LA company in Covington, LA, 40 miles to the north. John selected a location on Highway 190, the main road between Covington and Mandeville and the business thoroughfare for all of western St. Tammany parish (county). The site was just across Lake Pontchartrain from Southland's main operation, via world's longest bridge, the Causeway.

"Buck" Rogers, a good young warehouseman at Southland, was assigned to run the Covington warehouse. John hired a local truck driver in the last week of February, and they began to stock the branch from out of the Metairie inventory. The highly visible location paid off immediately, as several sales were made during the stocking process to passers-by.

Sales comfortably exceeded the breakeven estimate of $40,000 per month. Operating for essentially 10 months of 1977, sales averaged almost $50,000 per month and seemed to be accelerating before the typical seasonal slowdown from December to February.

VALUING THE BRANCH

In early 1978, John and his family began to discuss "spinning-off" the branch as a separate corporation, with John trading his partial ownership of Southland for complete ownership of the Covington operation (working title "Tammany Supply, Inc.").

In March 1978, Southland's accountant worked up a 1977 income statement for the Covington branch as if it had operated independently. She also, with John's input, projected the following three years' performance for valuation purposes. To complete the picture, she projected the value of the Covington assets on June 30, 1978, the day the sale would take place.

All that remained was to determine a selling price that John would find worth paying, and the accountant would consider in Southland's best interest. To insure fairness to all parties, it was decided that it would be an "arm's-length" transaction, that is, that John would pay a fair market price.

Southland would finance the inventory for one year, but the remainder of the sale would be cash. John could apply the value of his Southland stock, he would sell some real estate he owned, and borrow the rest from the bank.

The following is the statement presented to John by the accountant

Tammany Supply, Inc.					
Income Statement	Actual	>>>>>	>>>>>	>>>>>	Projected
	1977	1978	1979	1980	
Sales	496486	660000	720000	800000	
Cost of Goods Sold	394763	528000	576000	640000	
	20.5%	20.0%	20.0%	20.0%	Margin
Total Income	101723	132000	144000	160000	
		1.33	1.09	1.11	SalesIncr
Expenses:		0.98	0.95	0.92	EconScale
Personnel	42058	54791	56784	58046	
Operations	13041	16989	17607	17998	
Sales	6557	8542	8853	9050	
Administration	9225	12018	12455	12732	
Depreciation	2074	2702	2800	2862	
Total Expenses	72955	95043	98499	100687	
					AvgProfit
Profit/Loss BIT	28768	36957	45501	59313	$42,635

EARNINGS APPROACH

The average profit over one actual and three projected years will be the basis for valuation by the earnings approach. Let us look at desired returns of 16, 18 and 20%:

Earnings = Investment * Return on Investment, or

Investment = Earnings ($43,586) / Return (16,18, or 20%)

If we require a return of 20% on our investment, this level of earnings justifies a selling price of $217,930. Should we be able to live with 16%, we could pay $272,413. Let us settle on an 18% return, suggesting a value of $242,142, and look at other valuation methods.

BOOK VALUE

Since the transaction would be an asset purchase, let us look at the asset section of the balance sheet prepared by the accountant:

Expenses:	Adjust	1977	1978	1979	1980	
Personnel	-2000	40058	52186	54083	55285	
Operations	5.0%	13693	17839	18487	18898	
Sales	2.0%	6688	8713	9030	9231	
Administration	5.0%	9686	12619	13078	13368	
Depreciation		2074	2702	2800	2862	
Total Expenses		72199	94058	97479	99645	
						AvgProfit
Profit/Loss BIT		29524	37942	46521	60355	$43,586

Again, John is aware of adjustments that should be made to make the statement more accurate. He suspects that about $4,000 of the accounts receivable is uncollectible, and that inventory is about $6,000 over expressed. He also estimates that the fixed assets of the business have been depreciated to about $8,000 less than their replacement value. Adjusted book value is then:

Assets:	1978
Cash	22831
Accounts Receivable	85800
Collection Days	37.17
Inventory	118411
Turns	5.44
Other Assets	11733
Total Assets	$238,775

COMPOSITE

The market approach is not very appropriate here, since the characteristics of such a small firm are so much different from those for which price/earnings ratios would be reported. The large plumbing supply chains report p/e's of 8.5 to 12 on after tax earnings. A 20% tax rate on average earnings ($43,586), would leave $34,868; assuming a p/e for a small firm of 7, the market approach would yield a value of $244,076. Generally in valuations of this type, some composite of the earnings value ($242,142) and adjusted book ($236,775) is used. In this case, they are so close that it seems safe to use $240,000 as a fair market value.

 **PUT YOURSELF IN THEIR SHOES**

Is John underestimating the disadvantages of independence: decreased purchasing power; loss of access to the considerably larger inventory in the Metairie warehouse, and; management depth and other synergies due to being part of a larger operation?

- Can John assume that Southland's customers will become Tammany's customers? Why would they, or why might they not? Can TSI maintain the service level they had with South-land's resources behind them?

- John is 35 years old, and knows the administrative side of the business, but not the "pieces and parts;" Buck knows the material but now, at 20 years old, has become purchasing agent as well as warehouse manager. Are they in over their heads?

- Is an arms-length transaction feasible when the buyer has so much more information than the seller? Is John's suggested price going to be acceptable?

- Could the final price have been flexible, based on the first few years' performance of TSI? Should John have factored in the cyclical nature of the business, rather than counting on steady growth for the evaluation period?

- Do you agree with the evaluation process? What might you have done differently? Do you agree with the result? If you were to modify it, in which direction would you go? Should the deal happen? Is it "win-win?"

Negotiating the Sale

If we decide we want to buy a business, we should decide on a bargaining range before we go into the final negotiating session. If we cannot meet on price, perhaps concessions on payment terms could make up the difference. We should know the tax and legal consequences of our options. If the discussion takes us outside our range, we should schedule another session, and reanalyze the data. We must allow for the possibility that the deal cannot be made.

Ultimately we must decide whether the purchase, at a price that the seller will accept, gives us a better chance of success than starting from scratch in competition with the business. Perhaps the seller's errors would start us in a deficit position; we might prefer creating our own corporate culture and customer relationships; maybe we can find a better location, facility, newer equipment, etc. On the other hand, the cost of taking sufficient business away from existing firms could be ruinous.

With a marketing plan in place, we can refine our consideration further by beginning to make the very tangible decisions that allow us to test the feasibility of the venture. How many people will we need? What will we have to pay them? How much space will we need? What is it likely to cost? What are our equipment needs? What other operating expenses will there be?

What are our sales expectations? How do expenses vary with the level of sales? What level of sales will allow us to break even? How likely are we to achieve this? How long will it take?

Once we have identified a venture where the answers to these questions indicate promise, we must consider the alternative ways to seize the opportunity. We can choose to start a new business "from scratch," acquire a franchise, or purchase an existing business. The cost of bringing a new business to profitability must be compared to the higher expenses but potentially "surer" path to success of franchising, and to the purchase price and potential of an existing business.

Establishing the purchase price of a "going concern" can be particularly difficult. While there are alternative methods to quantifying a value from available data on the firm, the quality of that data is often suspect because it is provided by the seller.

Real Scenario 9:   Tammany Supply, Inc. (B)

Based on evaluations done by Southland Plumbing Supply, verified and fine-tuned by John Vinturella, John bought the assets of Southland's Covington, LA branch from his father and two brothers in mid-1978. Tammany Supply, Inc. was formed in June 1978, to begin operating on July 1, the effective date of the sale.

The branch had opened in early 1977 (see the "A" case), and had moderately exceeded expectations. In the spring of 1978 the business was evaluated, and a consensus was reached on a selling price of $240,000.

To pay for the branch's inventory, which represented about half of the sale value, John would apply his $65,000 worth of stock in the parent company and Southland would finance the remaining $55,000 over two years at market interest rate. For the other half of the sale value, John would pay $35,000 cash (from proceeds of the sale of some property he owned in Metairie), and pledge the $85,000 in accounts receivable to Southland. This would be paid monthly, as collected, with the remainder paid out in full at the end of the third month, collected or not.

While the terms may seem complicated, this structure was necessary to allow John to make the purchase. At 35 years old, John was risking all the assets he had accumulated in 12 years of working and investing, and any future inheritance (cashing in his Southland stock) on the success of TSI. Most of the remaining proceeds from the sale of the Metairie property were used for a down payment on a house in Covington, and a working capital loan to TSI ($25,000).

John's only other asset was his one-third ownership in the building in which TSI would operate. It was a former truck-repair garage that had been foreclosed on by an area bank; after a few months of renting the building, Southland was offered an attractive purchase price and terms by the bank. Instead, John and his brothers decided, for tax reasons, to form a partnership to buy it outside the corporation.

After receiving assurance from the bank that his credit history and the equity in the building supported his assuming the entire loan, John approached his brothers about a buyout. The building had appreciated some and was generating some income, requiring compensation in addition to assuming their share of the loan. They agreed on an amount, and with its payment John was now the sole owner of the building and its accompanying loan.

John unlocked the doors of TSI at 7am on July 1, 1978, hoping some customers would show up. He was in debt a half-million dollars, and his only chance of ever climbing out was to sell a lot of pipe and fittings.

START-UP TRAUMA

The long work-week required in serving the building trades was made even longer by having to catch up the administrative back-log after hours. For ten hours a day during the week and Saturday mornings, John was selling, serving customers, and directing ware-house and delivery operations. After hours, on Saturday afternoons, and frequently on Sundays, he was making bank deposits, paying bills, billing customers and making collection calls, writing purchase orders, and analyzing what was happening.

He had hired Bill, 10 years his senior, as a salesman but found he needed operations help more. Bill made the transition nicely, taking over purchasing as well as supervising the warehousemen. Bill would occasionally make outside sales calls, but increasing sales volume was less of a problem than servicing the customers that had already come to rely on TSI. Soon after, John hired Harry, 20 years his senior, to help with counter sales and bookkeeping.

With the added hands, and accompanying maturity, John could finish most of his work during working hours, and finally felt comfortable taking an occasional day off. Still, by 1980 John had not taken a real vacation since starting TSI, and it was time to assess where the business was headed and the best way to get there.

FIRST THREE YEARS

Sales comfortably exceeded expectations for the first three years at TSI.

By the end of 1980, John had paid off TSI's debts to Southland and to himself, and was beginning to draw a nice salary. The size of the staff had doubled since opening in 1978, and formed a hard-working and harmonious team. TSI was exceeding all the performance norms for the industry.

Following is a summary of financial performance for the period:

Tammany Supply, Inc.						
Income Statement	Actual	>>>>>	>>>>>	>>>>>	Projected	
	1977	1978	1979	1980		
Sales	496486	660000	720000	800000		
Cost of Goods Sold	394763	528000	576000	640000		
	20.5%	20.0%	20.0%	20.0%	Margin	
Total Income	101723	132000	144000	160000		
		1.33	1.09	1.11	SalesIncr	
Expenses:		0.98	0.95	0.92	EconScale	
Personnel	42058	54791	56784	58046		
Operations	13041	16989	17607	17998		
Sales	6557	8542	8853	9050		
Administration	9225	12018	12455	12732		
Depreciation	2074	2702	2800	2862		
Total Expenses	72955	95043	98499	100687		
					AvgProfit	
Profit/Loss BIT	28768	36957	45501	59313	$42,635	

The company had decided on a March 31 fiscal year end, so income for 1978 has been annualized (it was a 9-month fiscal year). Also, for each year indicated, year-end actually includes the first quarter of the following year. This year-end was chosen to coincide with the end of a traditionally slow period, greatly simplifying taking physical inventory on over 6,000 items.

The performance improvements over projections were due largely to TSI's broadening its concept of the plumbing supply customer from plumbing contractors only to the general public. Direct-to-user (DTU) sales are unpopular with contractors, but improved sales volume, and the higher margins of retail sales make them worth the criticism to a supply house.

MOVING TO THE NEXT LEVEL

By 1980, John found it necessary to expand and improve TSI's space. Building economies of scale were such that he tripled the size of the building, bringing in tenant companies in related but non-competitive businesses (carpeting, paint, appliances).

TSI became a distributor of Kohler plumbing products, the best in the industry (they had been buying Kohler indirectly through Southland before then). They built a state-of-the-art showroom, and began to advertise on local television. The warehouse was remodeled, and a mezzanine added. A fork-lift and new truck were purchased. Soon after, they were among the first to use a Radio Shack TRS-80, an early personal computer, for their billing, accounts receivable, and inventory control functions.

St. Tammany Parish was booming, and TSI was gearing up to service that boom. Two regional plumbing supply chains offered to buy the business, but John was not interested. One opened a small Covington branch in competition with TSI, but it barely lasted a year.

 **PUT YOURSELF IN THEIR SHOES**

- Was the purchase agreement with Southland really at "arm's length," or were concessions made to John that might not have been made to an outsider? Did the terms lower the effective selling price? Was Southland continuing to bear some of the risk of TSI's success?

- Was John overreaching his financial resources when he purchased the business? Should he have postponed the deal a year? Should he have retained the partnership in the building with his brothers? Did he leave himself any financial "cushion?" Would you have done the same?

- How do you explain the way in which performance exceeded projections? Was one year of operating experience enough to project sales for the next three years? Did John "lowball" his sales estimates to Southland? Should John offer a supplemental payment to Southland? Could John's actions as business owner been enough different from his actions as partner to explain the difference in performance?

- Are two years of growth and success (mid-1978 to mid-1980) enough to justify the large additional investment made in 1980? Should it have been done more stage-wise? Is the observed growth rate sustainable? What are the consequences of it not being? Discuss in terms of company investment, and John's personal investment (building expansion).

- What are the implications of the competition "discovering" the Covington market? Have any barriers to entry been erected? Why could TSI drive a larger competitor out of the market? After they left, do you think they had given up on the market entirely?

Chapter 5
The Business Plan

The purpose of a business plan is to recognize and define a business opportunity, describe how that opportunity will be seized by the management team, and to demonstrate that the business is feasible and worth the effort. Where implementation of the plan requires participation of lenders and/or investors, the plan must also clearly and convincingly communicate the financial proposal to the prospective stakeholders: how much you need from them, what kind of return they can expect, and how they can be paid back.

Many entrepreneurs insist that their business concept is so clear in their heads that the written plan can be produced after start-up; this attitude "short-circuits" one of the major benefits of producing the plan. "A realistic business plan might save you from yourself by persuading you to abandon a bad idea while your mistakes are still on paper," says Roger Thompson in Nation's Business.

Do many people need to be saved from themselves? Are many entrepreneurs so determined to go into business that they overlook or underestimate the potential pitfalls? Is that all bad? Can many business proposals stand the harsh light of skepticism?

Let us say we worked out the numbers on paper, and are convinced that we do not need to be saved from ourselves. Do we still need to write the plan? The discipline of writing a plan forces us to think through the steps we must take to get the business started, and, to "flesh out ideas, to look for weak spots and vulnerabilities," according to business consultant Eric Siegel. A well-conceived business plan can serve as a management tool to settle major policy issues, identify "keys to success," establish goals and check-points, and consider long-term prospects.

Who is the audience for it? Certainly, the plan is very useful if we are looking for investors or lenders. It is the primary tool used to convince prospective stakeholders that the idea is promising, the market is accessible, the firm's management is capable, serious and disciplined, and that the return on investment is attractive. But even if we can finance the venture ourselves, these are useful issues to address.

What are the elements of a good business plan, and how does it differ from a bad one? The appearance of the plan says something about its preparers. It should be professional, though not lavish, so as not to distract from its contents.

While the formats of business plans can be as varied as the businesses themselves, there are components that should appear in all plans. These include an executive summary, elements which describe the opportunity, elements which specify how the business will operate, an analysis of financial expectations, a closing summary, and any supporting documentation.

Let us discuss each of these in a little more detail, with an audience assumed to be a reader who might be a prospective investor or lender, a trusted professional advisor, or a friend whose business judgment we value.

(1)　"Packaging"

The cover and title page should contain company name, address, phone number, primary contacts, and the month and year of issue. Often, the issuers include a copy number to control circulation.

The executive summary introduces the opportunity, and contains highlights of the substantive sections. It should concisely explain the current status of the company, its products and/or services, benefits to customers, and summary financial performance data. Where investment is being solicited, it should also include the amount of financing needed, and how investors will benefit and harvest their gains. With all this information, this summary should still be held to two pages, to insure its being read, and must generate enthusiasm about the proposal to entice the reader to consider the entire plan.

The closing summary, or "wrap-up," is a shorter summary, more directed to what is being asked of the reader. Supporting documentation includes relevant marketing research, and financial details and statements behind the financial proposal.

(2)   Descriptive

In order to reasonably evaluate the business proposal, the reader needs some background on the proposed company, and the industry in which it will compete. A company mission statement can be an effective starting point in conveying the business concept. Also of interest are company goals, such as commitment to long-term results, innovation, productivity, and social responsibility.

Company information should also include the evolution of the business idea and the current stage of company development. The primary stakeholders and their roles should be discussed. Important accomplishments and milestones should be described.

Industry information should include the industry's size (such as total sales and profits), geographical dispersion, some history, and its current status. Competition should be discussed in terms of their offerings, market niches, and the extent of the threat to your proposed venture. The possible benefits of buying an existing business or acquiring a franchise should be evaluated. Quotes and statements from recent periodicals on the directions of the industry can be very useful. A projection of where the industry will be and your role in it over your planning horizon can be of considerable interest.

What are the significant factors affecting the market: cultural, attitudinal, demographic, legal, and technological? What are the trends in demand? What are the threats to the market?

The primary objective of this section is to convey your perception of the opportunity, and the relevance of the marketing research that convinced you that it is real and achievable. Of particular interest are the size of the market you will enter, your competitive advantage or unique strength, the company's "value adding" process, and market share expectations. These are the competitive issues in a strategic analysis, the full scope of which we will discuss later.

(3) Marketing

This section is essentially the marketing plan, which we discussed in Chapter 2. In this section, we need to clearly delineate our niche, and our distinctive competence. Investors are particularly interested in measuring the extent to which we are "market-driven;" the potential of the product's market, sales, and profit is more important than its appearance or technology.

- We begin by describing our target market. What business are we in? What are we selling? How well positioned are we to provide it? Who are our customers (age, income, etc.)? How many of them are there? Is the number growing? The better and more accurate our source of these answers, the more compelling our proposal will be.

- Our market research will often yield comments and statements from respected sources about buying patterns and trends; these can add strength to our statements. Where are our customers? How much do they buy? What are their motivators?

- How well does our product meet their needs? From whom do they buy now? How are they best reached? How will we get our product to the customer? How will we advertise and promote it? Is the market seasonal?

- Will we price our product as price leader, value leader, or prestige product? Is there any opportunity for a unique form of service or support? What market share can we reasonably expect? How long will it take us to get there?

- Are there any barriers to entry: patents, sources of supply, distribution channels, etc.? How strong is brand loyalty? Can a small independent company compete? How are prices set? How important is the "experience curve?" Are there barriers to exit?

(4)   Logistics

Location/Facilities

How much space do we need? How much equipment? What other facilities are important? Should we buy property and equipment or lease, which makes exit easier? How many employees do we need at startup? Is business location a significant factor? If so, what are our location criteria?

Location criteria can be applied at three levels: the city or metropolitan area; the neighborhood or section of town, and; a specific site. Is the city or section growing? How fast? Which parts? Is it strong in the demographics (age, income, etc.) critical to our success? Is it going "downhill?"

Specific sites within acceptable areas require a more detailed level of analysis.
- Is the area perceived as safe?
- How close are our competitors?
- How well are neighboring businesses doing?
- Is access easy? Parking available?
- Will there be zoning problems? Neighborhood resistance?

Legal Structure

The most common business structures are proprietorships, partnerships, and corporations. A proprietorship is simply a one-owner business. It is the most prevalent form (on the order of 70% of all businesses) because it is the simplest and least expensive to start.

A partnership is basically a proprietorship for multiple owners. Most are general partnerships, where each partner is held liable for the acts of the other partners. A limited partnership allows for general and limited partners; limited partners' liability is limited to their contributed capital.

The decision to enter a partnership should be based on whether or not you can "go it alone." The main reasons for people to feel they cannot are lack of money, skills, connections, and confidence. Are there other ways to address these needs?

If you chose to go into business with a partner, be sure to prepare a formal, written partnership agreement. This should address: the contribution each will make to the partnership, financial and personal; how business profits and losses will be apportioned; the salaries, and financial rights of each partner, and; provisions for changes in ownership, such as a sale, succession, or desire to bring in a new partner.

The corporation is a legal entity, separate from its owners. It is a more secure and better defined form for prospective lenders/investors. Incorporation is perceived as limiting the owner's liability, but personal guarantees are generally required whenever there is liability exposure.

The traditional form is called the C-Corporation. An S-Corporation is frequently preferable as a start-up form, since the losses expected in the early stages of the business may be applied to the owner's personal tax return. Other forms include: the LLC, or Limited Liability Corporation; Trusts, often for a specific time-frame or purpose, and; combinations of legal entities such as "Co-Ops "and joint ventures.

Enlist the legal and tax advice of the professionals as to which form suits your venture best.

Ownership Structure and Capitalization

Once the legal structure is decided upon, issues of distribution of ownership, and distribution of risks and benefits may be addressed. The primary decision to be made is whether the venture will be financed by the entrepreneur or whether there is a need for other stakeholders, and whether these stakeholders will be investors or lenders or some combination thereof.

The entrepreneur must keep the long-term in view. Shares of ownership may not seem very valuable at startup, but the entrepreneur could seriously regret having sold them so cheaply when the company prospers. On the other hand, borrowing for a new venture can be extremely difficult. The criteria for making decisions about capitalization are discussed at length in the financial section.

Human Resources

Many business plans are evaluated largely on the qualifications and commitment of the management team. The human resource plan must realistically assess the skills required for success of the venture, initially and over the long run, and match the skills and interests of the team to these requirements. Gaps must be filled with additional employees, learning activities, and/or consultants.

Once tasks are assigned, an effective responsibility structure must be designed. This structure would include the management of the organization, formal and informal advisors, and a board of directors. Methods of staying in touch with the market, such as association memberships and networking systems, can also be part of the human resource plan.

The Strategic Plan

Purpose

The strategic plan defines the company's "competitive edge," that collection of factors that sets the business apart from its competitors and promotes its chances for success. It requires a clear evaluation of the competitive business climate and an intimate knowledge of the market for the entrepreneur's product. The strategic plan "borrows" from other sections of the business plan those items which help to establish the venture's uniqueness, and some overlap will be observed.

Small businesses are not scale models of big businesses; they are characterized by resource poverty and dependence on a fairly localized market. Their greater vulnerability to the consequences of a lack of focus stresses the importance of their strategic plan.

(2)   Internal Factors

The foundation for the strategic plan is a clear mission statement for the venture. Addressing the following questions can develop this statement:

- What business am I in? The answer to this question is not as simple as it seems. A good example of an industry group that failed to take a broader view is the railroads. If they had viewed their business as transportation rather than trains-and-tracks, then the airlines would be named Union Pacific and Illinois Central.
- Whom is our product intended to satisfy?
- What customer needs are being satisfied?
- How are these needs being satisfied, that is, by which of our methods or products?

Other issues relevant to our internal analysis include identification of our corporate philosophy. Examples would be our commitment to employee fulfillment, quality management, partnership with customers and suppliers, and good corporate citizenship.

A primary company goal is frequently to maximize long-term stake-holder wealth. Secondary goals might include targets for market share, innovation, productivity, physical and financial resources, manager performance and development, worker performance and attitude, job satisfaction, and social responsibility.

An important strategic option is in how we price our product (as a price leader, value leader, or prestige product). Other options include the way in which we differentiate ourselves from the competition, and the particular subset of the market, or niche, we seek to serve.

Real Scenario 10:   Tammany Supply, Inc. (C)

Tammany Supply, Inc. (TSI), a plumbing supply distributor in Covington, LA, got off to a running start in mid-1978 (see the "B" case). The Vinturella family had tested whether the market was large enough to support a supply house by opening a branch of Southland Plumbing Supply, Inc. there in early 1977. John Vinturella, oldest member of the company's second generation, started up the branch, then negotiated a buyout with the rest of the family to operate it as a separate company, TSI. John became sole owner of TSI, and gave up his stake in Southland.

TSI exceeded $1million in sales in its first full year, 1979, $2 million in 1983, and $3 million the very next year. Pre-tax profits during this period approached $100,000 per year.

TSI's timing was fortuitous, opening just as its market area, western St. Tammany parish, was becoming the New Orleans suburb of choice for upscale professionals. TSI's marketing approach, unconventional by supply house standards, contributed to this success; they openly courted retail sales, even advertising on television. By the time other supply houses began to look covetously at the market, TSI was firmly established. Their pre-emptive strike, opening before the opportunity was obvious, had created a barrier to others' entry.

THE "CRASH"

A more serious barrier to entry arose in 1985. The collapse of world oil prices took a devastating toll on the Louisiana economy, and the high-end suburb of the state's largest metropolitan area was particularly hard-hit. While TSI showed only a slight sales decrease in 1985, and a profit increase, the bottom fell out the next year. Sales fell almost 40% in 1986, and even lower in 1987.

TSI showed a profit on operations in 1986, barely half that of the year before, but did not charge off any of its looming credit losses. The homebuilding industry runs largely on credit, and depends on a steady or growing demand. When that demand falls off, builders are left with unsold houses and huge interest payments; contractors do not get paid, and cannot pay for their materials. TSI paid for its goods before it sold them, so it had no one to help it share the pain.

When most of TSI's bad-debt losses were written off in 1987, the operating loss for the year exceeded $100,000.

It was obvious that changes in the external environment had caused a need for reevaluating TSI's strategy, and the sense of free-fall to the company's fortunes made this need seem immediate.

WHAT DO WE DO NOW?

The options available to TSI were limited by the size of their market, the condition of the local economy, and their resource position. Inventory had shot up in 1984, in response to the higher level of business, and the increased sales raised accounts receivable accordingly. By 1985, the slowdown was becoming apparent, and TSI was beginning to get its inventory down, while stepping up collections to improve its cash position (see Figure 3).

Cash was sufficient at the end of 1987, $70,000 or so above usual levels, to support some diversification. This could take the form of additional inventory items, or the startup of some new operation. Related businesses were considered for the vacant spaces in TSI's building created by the collapse of appliance and ceiling fan stores. But could TSI succeed where so many homebuilding dependent businesses in the area were failing? Should they enter a field unrelated to construction?

In any case, TSI's core business had shrunk by 40%. Expenses could be cut some, but to cut them enough to matter would have left the company considerably less than a full-service supply house, and much more vulnerable to competition. John was also reluctant to cut TSI's excellent work force, even though they were working well below capacity.

Adding to John's problems with keeping TSI viable was the problem of meeting mortgage payments on a building that was now barely half occupied. Replacement tenants were nowhere to be found, and TSI could hardly bear to absorb the rental shortfall.

TSI's options were few, and decidedly unattractive. They could return the building to the bank and negotiate a lower monthly payment as a renter. They could downsize their payroll to a level appropriate to sales volume. Or, they could try to apply the vacant space and under-utilized human resources to generate some added sales volume and profits; the challenge lay in deciding how.

PUT YOURSELF IN THEIR SHOES

- Did decisions made during the good times contribute to the difficulty of dealing with the crash? Could the assets have been managed better? Could adjustments have been made more smoothly?

- Should the bad times ahead have been foreseen by TSI management? Were they slow to respond? Were their actions appropriate? Effective?

- Why is John so reluctant to scale the business down to a level appropriate to sales? What would the longer-term consequences be? How would the competition view such a move? What would it do to the chances for recovery as the economy improves?

- What are TSI's strategic options? What information would you gather to help evaluate possible new product lines or related ventures? What new offerings would fit well with traditional plumbing supply lines? Is it better to sell more things to existing customers, or bring in new customers?

- If new lines are added, is it better to re-train existing personnel or replace some with new employees experienced in the new line? If the re-train option is chosen, how long might it be before TSI can effectively market the new products?

- How effectively can TSI broaden its offerings with $70,000 in cash? What other options exist to leverage this cash, or generate more? Would it be better to preserve the cash to ride out the difficult period? Is this any time for "adventurism," or should John concentrate on holding on to what is left of his core business?

- How does John's ownership of the building, outside of TSI, affect his options? Is he caught in any conflict of objectives? Would he act differently on behalf of TSI if the building were owned by someone else? Should he try to sell the building?

- Is now the time to sell the business? Are the regional chains likely to still be interested? How fast can the business be "turned around?" What would you do?

External/Competitive Environment

Once we have set internal objectives, we must examine the external and competitive environments in which we will be trying to achieve them. The external environment consists of those factors which are largely outside our control, but affect the market for our product.

Examples of these factors include general economic conditions, regulations, technological developments, and consumer demographics and attitudes. This environment is very dynamic, but some attempt must be made at projecting its changes.

Analysis of the competitive environment must begin with consideration of whether there are any barriers to the entry of a new competitor into the market. How strong is consumer loyalty to existing brands? How important are economies of scale; can a small independent firm compete? Are capital requirements prohibitive? Is there some proprietary technology that puts prospective entrants in a serious competitive disadvantage? Is access to raw materials or to distribution channels limited in some way? Are new entrants limited by permit restrictions or regulations?

The competitive structure of the industry is another important consideration. Are there a few dominant firms, or is the industry fairly fragmented? Will current competitors attempt to "punish" new entrants, such as through a price war, heavy advertising, or exercising their clout with key suppliers? Is there some geographic niche we can serve? What factors create cost advantages or disadvantages? How important is a firm's position on the learning and experience curves? How are prices set? Is demand rising, even, or falling? Are there exit barriers that raise the risk of entry?

Relative strengths of our strategic partners must also be considered. What is the bargaining power of suppliers? How wide is our choice of suppliers? Is it costly for us to switch? Can our suppliers compete with us for the same customers? How important is our industry to our suppliers?

Do buyers have a wide choice of vendors? Can they make our product themselves? Are there less expensive or superior substitutes to our product in some segments of the market?

SWOT Analysis
(Strengths/Weaknesses/Opportunities/Threats)

The major strength of a company is that which most clearly distinguishes it from the competition, referred to as its "distinctive competence." It can take many forms, but it must be identified and built upon.

This competitive advantage can be in a primary aspect of the business (manufacture, sales, service), or a secondary one (support, personnel, purchasing, etc.). It is the critical factor in the company's value-adding process.

While the venture's weaknesses need not be emphasized, they should be recognized and identified. A plan to overcome them, or at least minimize their impact, is far more credible than denying that they exist.

Certainly, the opportunity addressed initially is central to the business plan, but a discussion of peripheral and/or future opportunities demonstrates a deeper understanding of the full range of possibilities of the venture. These can include a broader geographic area, wider product line, and new applications for current products.

Just as weaknesses must be recognized, so must threats to the future success of the business. These can be internal, such as a concept which can be easily copied, or limitations of working capital. Threats can also be external, such as an economic downturn, shifting demographics, or technological developments. Competitive factors can also come into play, such as entry of a major company in a related business.

The Financial Plan

(1)   Forecasting

The sales forecast "scales" the business. It determines the amount of people, space and equipment the venture will require which in turn can be related to financial requirements. While forecasting is an uncomfortable process for most people, an orderly approach can make it seem less like guesswork.

Unit sales and expected selling price can be estimated and extended to yield sales dollars. Comparative information adds credibility and perspective; government and trade association publications can be productive sources.

Key questions to ask ourselves are: How big is the market? Is it growing? What share can we reasonably expect? How long will it take us to get there? Often, separate statements are produced for optimistic, expected, and pessimistic (OEP) projections.

Industry norms for gross margin can be adapted to our concept to yield gross margin dollars. We must then estimate our cost structure. The following section discusses how this might be done. Again, industry norms modified by our experience and concept of operation can be very useful.

At this point, a break-even analysis can be performed. Fixed costs, or those which are independent of our sales level, should be separated from variable costs for the analysis.

Does the market potential support the break-even sales level? Where does this sales level fall within our OEP spectrum? Should we proceed if break-even requires our most optimistic sales projection? Should we re-examine our numbers? Which can be changed or improved (sales, margins, expenses)? Should we suffer some margin to increase sales? Can expenses be cut?

2)   The Pro Forma Income Statement

In the early stages of the business, sales are going rapidly (we hope!) from zero to some expected level over several months; initial marketing efforts may take 6 months to dent the public awareness. For a pre-startup income statement to accurately represent this high state of flux, it is recommended that it show performance by month for the first three years, or until profitability is achieved.

The income section of the statement shows the sales estimate and cost of goods sold (CGS), and the difference - generally referred to as gross margin dollars, or margin. CGS is generally expressed as a percentage of sales. Margin dollars are then available to pay expenses, with the remainder being the before-tax profit. See Tammany Supply Case A for an example of this process.

Categories for the expense section of the statement can be grouped into: personnel; administrative; sales expense, and; operations. Methods of allocation between these groups can vary widely, but this structure is useful for considering the form our expenses will take.

Personnel expenses consist of salaries (often split into "Officers" and "Others") and related costs, such as payroll taxes and benefits. These costs are sometimes apportioned to the other groups based on person-nel functions.

Administrative costs can include accounting and legal expenses, bad debt and collection costs, bank charges, depreciation, and interest. Estimation of interest paid is iterative, that is, the amount to be bor-rowed must be estimated, yielding a number for interest expense; this is part of the profit/loss picture, which determines how much must be borrowed. Seldom are more than 2 or 3 passes required to converge to a final estimate, and spreadsheet programs make the process simple.

Sales expenses include advertising and promotion, and sales commis-sions. Operations costs are such things as rent, vehicle expense, utilities, and supplies.

For the purposes of estimation, it is best to use the detailed categories to come up with numbers that we can "sink our teeth into." These can then be consolidated into the above groupings when the business enters more of a "steady-state."

In building a spreadsheet pro forma income statement, we are building a "model" of the business. It should be constructed using relationships rather than constant values, such as margin and some expense categories as a percent of sales, sales increases with time as a percentage growth, etc. Then we can experiment with a range of reasonable alternatives for our "control variables," such as estimated sales, and profit margins.

(3)   The Pro Forma Balance Sheet

Whereas the income statement describes company performance over some period of time, such as a month or year, the balance sheet shows the value of the company at a point in time (opening day, end of the fiscal year). This value is expressed as the value of the company's assets, and its liabilities, with the difference being net worth or owners' equity.

Assets are classified as "Current" or "Other." Current assets include cash and "liquid" investments such as certificates of deposit, and items (relatively) readily converted to cash, such as inventory and accounts receivable. Often the values presented account for a portion of inventory being obsolete, and a portion of accounts receivable being uncollectible, but this is not applicable to startup ventures. Other assets are primarily "Fixed," that is, have some relatively long service life over which their value is amortized. These include property and improvements, vehicles, and equipment. Depreciation schedules are generally "aggressive," taking maximum advantage of tax law, and frequently cause fixed asset values to be understated.

Liabilities are generally classified as "Current" and "Long-Term." Current liabilities consist of items due in the relatively short term, such as accruals of sales and payroll taxes, and "Accounts Payable," or invoices for goods received. Long-term liabilities are generally "Notes Payable" with fixed repayment terms.

The difference between assets and liabilities, as though the company were being liquidated, is the net worth of the business, or "Owners' Equity." The balance sheet must be consistent with the income statement. Accumulated profits become gain in equity, purchases become assets, note payments decrease loan balances, depreciation reduces asset values.

See Tammany Supply Case B for an example of a summary Balance Sheet.

(4) Capital Requirements

The capital requirements of the business can be developed as the sum of: pre-startup outlay; fixed assets needed within the startup period, and; accumulated operating losses until break-even or better is achieved. The requirement is generally met by some combination of cash and loans; we will discuss sources of funds in the next section.

Determination of the capital required for a successful startup is an iterative process, greatly simplified by spreadsheet programs. Appended to the bottom of the income statement spreadsheet can be a cash flow section, showing cash in, plus profit or less loss, is equal to cash out. Actually two adjustments are required to this nominal equation: depreciation must be added back in, because it is a non-cash expense, and; the principal portion of a note payment must be subtracted, because it does not affect expenses but does "transform" cash into equity.

What is needed in the pre-startup period? Generally there are fixed assets required, primarily the property from which we will operate or the cost of modifying leased property for our purposes, with the next largest commitment being equipment. We must open with an appropriate level of inventory. There are probably some salary, supplies, and other expenses associated with setting up to open.

Some of these are "sunk" costs, that is, unrecoverable even if we shut the business down. Others can be recovered only at "fire-sale" rates on shutdown. These losses may be considered exit costs, and may be thought of as the minimum loss should the venture not "get off the ground."

Still many entrepreneurs manage to find the means to fund their ventures. The National Federation of Independent Businesses reports that about 20% of all businesses start on less than $5,000, and nearly half with less than $20,000.

Other fixed assets may be needed after opening for business, but before profitability is reached. To the extent that we can delay their acquisition without harming our business prospects, we can lessen our capital requirements. Often we can lease equipment, sometimes with credit towards later purchase, until our longer-term needs become clearer.

Pre-startup outlays and equipment needs are fairly tangible and easy to conceptualize, but the other component of our capital requirements needs is more difficult to estimate. The amount of our accumulated operating losses depends on sales and expense estimates reaching well into the future.

One way to estimate accumulated operating losses (AOL) is to run our model with a zero starting cash amount, and scan month-ending cash until this balance reaches its most negative, that is before profitability begins to turn the balance back upward. This most negative value is our best estimate of AOL, and our starting cash must be this amount plus some contingency "cushion."

We now have all the components of our capital requirement, and it is important that we not "cut it too close." Some conservatism must be applied to the model, and some contingencies allowed for. We want to provide enough to make the business a long-term success; potentially profitable businesses often close because of being "starved" for operating capital in the startup period.

It is also important to document the assumptions made in arriving at our estimates, and to establish milestones and landmarks for our financial performance to "calibrate" it against expectations; it is much harder to be objective about how we are doing once into the venture and possibly even faced with whether it is worth the effort to continue. Where there are investors or lenders involved, part of their financial commitment to the venture may be contingent on reaching these milestones.

Once capital requirements are established, we must consider whether we can fund the startup ourselves. Otherwise, we now enter the fundraising stage.

(5)   Sources of Funds

While the discussion of capital requirements may have seemed pessimistic, with its mention of exit costs and deciding when to "pull the plug," pessimism is what the entrepreneur at fundraising will be greeted with. It is the entrepreneur's dream, about which he or she has great difficulty being objective, being presented to skeptical prospective stakeholders, that is investors and lenders. They have seen several ventures fail, but never have they seen an entrepreneur who allowed for that possibility in advance. What would it say to them if that possibility were acknowledged?

Stakeholders generally expect a substantial financial commitment to the venture by the entrepreneur. Their sense is that it should not be easy for the entrepreneur to give the venture a half-hearted try, leaving the consequences of failure to the stakeholders. The entrepreneur's financial commitment (EFC) is often a combination of personal funds and investments and loans from "friendly" sources, that is family and friends.

Assuming then an EFC of 50%, what are our options for raising the other half of our capital requirement? The basic decision to be made is how much will be raised by selling equity, that is shares of ownership in the venture, and how much will be borrowed.

To the entrepreneur, the advantage of using equity financing is that the investor is sharing the risks of the venture, and that this lowers expenses since there is no debt service to be paid. The investor also shares the rewards, however, and the entrepreneur must be careful not to sell the equity too cheaply.

What do we have to offer prospective investors? For most, their primary interest is in a high return on their investment, through dividends and appreciation. Other considerations might be opportunities for tax benefits, and for director and consulting income. Of generally lesser interest are non-cash rewards, such as privileged information, access to new products, and "psychic income." There is little appeal to most investors in being a long-term minority owner in a closely-held business, so some way of "cashing out," such as a provision for company buy-back, must be offered.

How do we identify prospective investors? We could sell stock to the public. The Initial Public Offering (IPO) is seldom an option for startups, however, unless they have a high growth potential proprietary product. The high costs involved make about $10 million the minimum feasible IPO; more often they are in the $50-100 million range.

Less visible as a source of startup capital are individual investors, known as "angels," who typically invest $20,000 to $100,000 in private companies. Angels are thought to represent a pool of risk capital in excess of $30 billion each year.

While stakeholders are hard to find at startup, sources of assistance are available. A good starting point is the U.S. Small Business Administration (SBA). Their Small Business Investment Company (SBIC) program allows private investment partnerships, or SBICs, to leverage their capital using SBA guarantees.

Debt financing, on the other hand, adds to our fixed costs, but makes no claim beyond the amount of the debt no matter how great our success. Standards for debt financing are generally very difficult for startups to meet; lenders are not generally willing to share the risk with you. If you are turned down by a lender, ask them for specific reasons.

If the reasons cannot be countered with this lender, the insight gained can be used to strengthen the presentation to the next.

A credit line, which we draw upon only as needed, can be used to hold down interest costs. Easy payment terms from suppliers of startup inventory can lower borrowing requirements. Assets of the business can be used as collateral, but a personal guarantee will almost always be required. This commits your personal assets to repayment of the loan.

(6)   Finance Plan

Is startup capitalization adequate? Is it used well? Are all startup costs recognized? Are sales projections credible? Achievable? Are sales and sales growth expectations realistic?

Are expense estimates reasonable? Complete? Are margin goals realistic? Convincing? Is there a solid basis for estimates (industry norms, experience), or do they appear to be guesswork?

Is the progression of income/expense estimates credible? Are income, cash flow, and balance statements consistent? Is cash well managed? Is the cash management strategy clear? Does the total package (text, statements, assumptions, etc.) present a clear and complete picture of the financial position?

(7)   Presentations

Are you well-rehearsed and comfortable with the content? Does your delivery convey professionalism and enthusiasm?

Is the presentation clear and concise? Does it stress benefits to the prospect? Is it attractive and interesting? Does it end with a call to action?

The following Real Life Scenario continues our consideration of the development of Tammany Supply, Inc. It refers to a business plan which is included in the Appendix. While this plan concerns a "mid-course correction" rather than a startup, it serves as a good example of the business plan principles which we have discussed.

Elements of Style

Now that we have all the components of the business plan laid out, we can begin to craft the final product. Some "first impressions" criteria for a good business plan are that it be attractive and interesting, well organized and carefully edited, and easy to understand.

Readers must be led through our analysis in a way that leads them to accept our conclusions. Our primary objective is to convey that there is an opportunity, that we are equipped to seize it, and that "the numbers work." It is helpful to be concise and focused, and to avoid vague and/or unsubstantiated claims. Potential problems must be anticipated and addressed, leading to a convincing likelihood of success. Projections must be rigorously realistic and objective, and based on reasonable assumptions.

- M. John Storey, principal of Storey Communications, suggests that we: "Keep the plan incredibly simple. Talk in pictures. Back up your images with a phone-book-size financial package, but only at the end. Never allow a reader to say 'Too complicated, not for me,' on the first page." He also cautions that we "leave out the mumbo-jumbo," keeping the focus on "who's going to buy what product, and at what price?" He urges the use of summaries to help plant the key facts in a prospective investor's mind: profit, potential, costs, key customers.

- Katie Muldoon, president of Muldoon & Baer, suggests that the plan, which she views as a prospectus, should reflect your personality and ambitions: "Investors bet on people, and the prospectus is an opportunity to sell your qualities. Make sure the writing reflects your drive and professionalism." She adds that "It's like any other selling job. You've got to know your audience, write to your audience."

- A. David Silver of ADS Financial Services suggests that "lenders and investors are more interested in tenacious entrepreneurs than in relaxed or casual" ones. He cautions, though, that you "balance your persistence, so that you don't appear 'pushy'."

"Deal killers" can include: carelessness in preparation (what does this convey?); insufficient belief in the project by its principals, and; a lack of comfort with and confidence in the company principals on the part of prospective stakeholders. More often, business proposals fail for more tangible reasons, such as: success depending on too many or too shaky contingencies; an inadequate return to justify the risks, and; the absence of a "graceful way out," that is a credible exit strategy, for stakeholders.

Where we are seeking financial stakeholders, we would like to get the opportunity to present the highlights of our proposition in person. While a request for an oral presentation could be met with resistance,

Oral presentations are generally characterized by a very short time allowance, and a somewhat skeptical audience. Make your case quickly; Storey suggests that you should be able to explain the business opportunity in 25 words or less, leading them to suggest "tell me more." Tell the prospect what's in it for them, particularly what benefits they will enjoy if they invest.

The oral presentation must answer many of the same questions as the written; it can be more difficult due to time constraints, or easier because we have more senses to appeal to. Computer presentation packages can be used to generate attractive, professional visual aids. Do not use copies of spreadsheets or printed pages as visuals; design "pithy" slides that are not too "busy." Use the visuals as an outline of your talk so that you do not have to refer to notes. Be sure to adapt your presentation to the medium, and to your audience.

Rehearse your presentation until you are very comfortable with it. Present it to a knowledgeable and objective friend for feedback. Time it to make sure you do not overstay your welcome.

Corporate trainer and speaker Lani Arredondo suggests the AMMA rule for presentations, that they be: attention-getting; meaningful; memorable, and; activating. She stresses that the purpose of a presentation is to persuade. She cautions that: perception is more powerful than fact; people are inundated with data, and; people forget fast.

A presentation must be balanced between information elements and relational ones, those that relate to your audience. Ideally, the presentation should lead directly into the prospect asking how they can participate.

Summary

We can evaluate our business plan according to the following checklist:

(1)   General

- Is it clear what business the company is in? Is the concept well thought out? Expressed effectively?
- Is the overall presentation concise, businesslike? Is the plan attractive? Well-written? Interesting?
- Does the plan "sell"? Generate enthusiasm?

(2)   Marketing Plan

- How good is the market research?
- How applicable is it to this specific business?
- How well do the principals understand the industry?
- Is the target market clearly identified?
- Is it the right market?
- Is it big enough?
- Is it growing?
- Is the marketing approach credible and convincing?

(3)   Strategic Issues

Is the business sufficiently differentiated? Is its competitive advantage clear and convincing? Is product positioning and pricing appropriate to the competitive situation?

- Are company strengths sufficient for success?
- Are any company weaknesses fatal?
- Are all promising opportunities recognized?
- Are all-significant threats adequately considered?
- Are the human resources indicated sufficient to the task? Used well?
- Is the scope of operations appropriate to the opportunities?
- Are the keys to success clearly identified?

(4)   Overall

Is the plan convincing? Are the principals realistic about the industry's direction and the competitive situation, and reasonable in their projections? Are they capable of implementing the plan?

TIME OUT! - YOUR COACH SAYS

1. What is the major purpose of a business plan? Is a business plan needed where you can finance the venture yourself?
2. What is the basis of the financial plan? How can we forecast sales? How can we test projections for reasonability? How do we determine the capital requirements of a venture?
3. On what basis will you choose which venture finance to consider?

From its 1978 startup through 1985, Tammany Supply, Inc. (TSI) of Covington, LA was the dominant plumbing supply wholesaler in western St. Tammany parish. St. Tammany, an upscale suburb of New Orleans, was one of the country's fastest growing counties during this period, and TSI's growth rate reflected it.

Sales evened off in 1985, then fell precipitously in 1986 as the collapse of world oil prices took the energy out of the Louisiana economy. Sales fell even further in 1987 as TSI suffered its first money-losing year (see the "C" case).

New residential construction, which had been a mainstay for TSI, fell off dramatically as homes were left vacant all over the parish by people leaving Louisiana to find work. TSI had to perform a re-evaluation of their strategy, and do it fast, to cope with a 40% decrease in their core business.

DIVERSIFICATION

As the "crash" damages to TSI were being assessed, its president, John Vinturella, began to write the company's first formal business plan. This plan consisted primarily of a strategic analysis and an implementation plan to get TSI back to profitability. The 1987-89 plan served as a road map for the way back, with some mid-course corrections made in a 1988 update; the 1990-92 plan was a bit more comprehensive, since the air of crisis had been removed. The effectiveness of that plan serves to illustrate that planning is not just for startups, but is an ongoing process.

The following excerpt from the plan describes the recovery strategy:

"The decreased demand was addressed on three fronts: the impact on sales volume was softened by diversifying product lines, cash was preserved by a gradual selling off of inventory, and expenses were cut.

Diversification of product lines was intended to increase retail sales, particularly in remodeling and add-on items. To that end the company began emphasizing spas and whirlpools, and became a master distributor for Toro sprinkler systems. In 1987 TSI opened the Outdoor Living Center (OLC), a retailer of outdoor and patio furniture and accessories. In 1988 the company opened a franchise of Singer Kitchens and Baths (SKB), strengthening its cabinet sales effort and adding appliances. In 1989 the company broadened its water treatment and air-conditioning supply offerings.

Less glamorous, but just as vital were the inventory reduction and cost-cutting campaigns. Low turnover items were returned to the manufacturer or offered to other suppliers and the public at break-even pricing or less. Staff was reduced by attrition, one truck was retired, insurance was tightened, and some functions previously contracted out were brought back in."

By the 1991 update, a preliminary report on results could be made:

"The last three years have seen the end of "free☐fall," as business stabilized but did not really improve. Sales volume is recovering, but margins have remained weak; 1988 was a moderately good year, 1989 a moderately bad one, and 1990 was essentially break-even."

Note: Minor discrepancies may be noted between the financial data in the business plan, and that reported in this series of cases. Data in the plan is based on statements generated by TSI, whereas data in the cases is based on tax returns, and reflects accounting adjustments that improve accuracy. None of the differences are large enough to affect the discussions of strategy.

Some mid-course correction was called for:

"At the end of 1990, by mutual agreement, TSI turned the SKB store over to the franchiser. SKB continues to operate the store, and TSI is out of the cabinet business.

Despite our high hopes for the kitchen business, it did not create as good a fit with our overall operation as we had hoped, and the attractive margins were eaten up by heavy personnel demands.

The result of this decision is a slight downsizing of our operation.... In 1990, SKB sales represented almost 15% of TSI sales."

Some good news could be found:

"On the positive side, we feel that we can make up this volume in our mainstream business. We see a definite increase in construction activity, and our two local competitors left the area in October 1990."

The local competitors referred to were Park Supply, a Picayune MS company which opened a Covington branch in 1986, and Plumbing Specialty of New Orleans which entered the market in 1988. All was not quiet on the competitive front, however; Southern Pipe, a regional chain based in Meridian MS, announced in early 1991 that they would open a western St. Tammany branch by the end of the year.

PERFORMANCE

Since TSI could hardly survive another year like 1987, the following three years were projected to be the recovery period. It was a spotty recovery at best. Sales drifted upward, exceeding $2 million again by 1990. Of the three, only 1988 was profitable, and would not have been but for a large income tax refund reflecting the huge loss of the previous year.

Still, some cause for optimism could be found:

"We hope that the worst is behind us. All reasonably question-able debts are written off and expenses are tightly controlled. State and area economic outlook have improved, and the local recovery seems to have some strength."

Projections for 1991-92 show an expectation of a return to profitability on the order of $30,000 per year.

 **PUT YOURSELF IN THEIR SHOES**

- Was 1987 too late for TSI to write its first business plan? Would a formal written strategic plan in 1985 have helped guide the company through the difficult period? Could it have helped soften the impact? What was the purpose of the 1990 plan?

- Evaluate the strategic plan. Does the assessment of external forces seem reasonable? Are internal capabilities reasonably assessed? Does the strategy selection follow logically from the assessments?

- Are the goals expressed too modest, reasonable, or too ambitious? Are they relevant to the problems facing TSI? Are the tools necessary to their accomplishment identified?

- Is management in control and on target? Are they collecting the right information, and evaluating it properly, as a guide to future actions?

- How successful has the diversification strategy been? Should it be abandoned, or simply refined? Do the reasons for drop-

ping SKB make sense? How is SKB significantly different
from the other forms of diversification?

- Why did two competitors move in after the crash? Why do you
  think they could not make it? Why were the earlier entries
  small independents, while the regional chain waited until an
  apparent recovery was under way? What effect do you expect
  the 1991 entry of a competitor with "deep pockets" will have
  on TSI's recovery?

- Are you confident about TSI's prospects for the remaining two
  years of this planning period? What would you do differently?

Chapter 6
Family Business

Family Business Review defines a family business as "... *a business in which the members of a family have legal control over ownership.*"   By this definition, family business is widely acknowledged to be the predominant form of business organization in the industrialized world.

According to the National Family Business Association, 90% of U.S. businesses are family controlled, producing half of the GNP and employing half of the work force. While small businesses are generally family businesses, the opposite is not necessarily the case; more than a third of Fortune 500 firms are controlled by families.

Why the Current Interest?

Generational factors and the decline of the corporation have combined to create a new focus on family business.

As post-war entrepreneurs have retired, control of many companies has passed from one dominant individual to power-sharing arrangements between siblings and cousins. Changes in ownership have accompanied these changes in control. Consequently, we are in the early stages of the greatest intergenerational transfer of wealth in United States history.

In addition to generational factors, other changes in the workplace are helping to raise the visibility of family businesses. We frequently see references to the frustrations of corporate life - glass ceilings, restructuring, downsizing, rigid bureaucracies and unyielding corporate cultures. Family business, seen in the past as provincial and behind the times, is now being viewed in a different light. At the same time, the importance of smaller businesses to our global competitiveness, innovativeness, and to job creation has begun to be recognized.

Basic Strengths and Weaknesses of the Family Business Structure?

The strengths are described by Robert G. Donnelley in a classic article in the Harvard Business Review (Donnelley, 1964): "the availability of otherwise unobtainable financial and management resources because of family sacrifices; important community and business relationships stemming from a respected name; a dedicated and loyal internal organization; an interested, unified management-stockholder group; a sensitivity to social responsibility; and continuity and integrity in management policies and corporate focus."

In order to capitalize on these strengths, family business principals must understand the impact of the family on the business, identify and address potential areas of conflict, create a shared vision, and implement that vision through communications, planning, and policies. The greatest weakness of the family business structure is that family communication often leaves too much unsaid.

It is dangerous to assume that all family members share a business vision, while avoiding the hard work of communicating and understanding each member's goals and ambitions and developing an implementation process that works for everyone. To illustrate, we have invited a guest perspective, which appears at the end of this chapter.

Issues Unique to Family Business

Family firms must, of course, deal with the same economic and competitive factors as other businesses. Relationship problems among owners, managers and employees exist in all firms. But in the family firm, another set of issues overlays these and creates additional opportunities for conflict.

In order to facilitate our consideration of typical family business issues and problems, we will base our discussions on a hypothetical firm, an insurance agency:

Real Scenario 11:   The Peterson Agency - History

Wes Peterson returned to Cincinnati after a Navy stint during the Korean War, and took a job selling insurance with a local independent insurance agency. The owner, who was considering retirement when Wes started, had no natural successor and offered to sell the business to Wes. The purchase was a real stretch for Wes, but he thoroughly enjoyed the business and took the chance.

Wes was very personable, and active in church and civic activities, and rather quickly built up a substantial clientele. Still, building a business while raising a growing family and making payments to the previous owner generated a lot of stress for the young veteran.

But Wes was patient, and focused on the long-term success of the business. With hard work and a sincere concern for his customers' best interests, his reputation for service and ethical behavior spread and the business grew beyond his most optimistic projections.

After 4 years of financial struggle, he became comfortable that he had built a lasting business. But this comfort did not lead to complacency.

Wes continued to broaden and update his offerings, and the Peterson Agency became a full-service financial planning firm. On the 25th anniversary of his taking over the business, his employees gave him a surprise party; after several cries of "Speech!," Wes reflected on his career choice and hopes for the future:

"Thank you, but it is you who deserve most of the credit. Together we have changed many people's concept of the insurance agency from seller of insurance to adviser in assuring their lifetime financial security. We have converted contacts to clients and then to friends. I am confident that we have never taken advantage of the trust that has been shown in us.

"As my children begin to take some of the load off of this old man, I can assure you that our commitment to our basic principles, putting our customers first and investing in staying as creative and up-to-date as we can be, will not waver. But this is all too serious for this occasion; let the celebration resume!"

Wes then began to "work the room," expressing his appreciation individually to every employee for their contribution to the firm's success.

Some of the Issues

This is a fairly typical situation: a business begun in the 1950s, by a male, and brought to stability with some financial hardship. After a period of substantial growth, the entrepreneur welcomes the entry of the expected next generation of leadership.

Note the similarity of the Peterson Agency's basic strengths to those outlined by Donnelley: financial sacrifices, community relationships, dedicated and loyal organization, and high ethical standards.

In a recent study by Family Business magazine, 48% of the family businesses surveyed used their name as the company name. Of those companies bearing the family name, 20% of respondents made "respect for the name" one of their top three business priorities compared to 9% of the others.

Our story of the Peterson Agency begins at a critical time in the life cycle of family businesses. The company is a mature one, still clearly run by its founder. It has grown to a comfortably profitable size, but its growth is now limited by the founder's hands-on style. The staff is well-treated and well-compensated, but all planning, direction and policy-making come from the founder. Generally self-taught in business, the founder is authoritative, financially conservative, and a bit of a "workaholic."

Let us now examine Wes' family situation, again with an eye toward typical family business issues, and update our story to the present:

Real Scenario 11:   The Peterson Agency - Family Background

        When Wes left the Navy, he married his high-school sweetheart, Eleanor Clark. "Ellie" had just finished nursing school and the income from her nursing practice would help them get established until their first child was born. Susan arrived just before Wes bought the insurance agency, with Harley and then Matthew following on a two-year cycle. While Ellie enjoyed the nursing profession, her first maternity leave turned out to be permanent. By the time Matthew was born, they did not need the added income, and three little ones kept her busy enough.

All three children worked in the family business during their school years, doing menial tasks for which the company essentially paid their allowance. To a large extent, Wes "programmed" the children's attitudes toward the business; his choice of assignments for Susan emphasized the drudgery of the everyday routine, while he spoke enthusiastically about the rewards of the business to his sons.

As Susan neared the end of high school, she had become quite an asset to the office operation but showed no interest in returning to the business after college. She later earned a Ph.D. in Management and became a college professor. Harley was the serious and responsible son, anxious to learn the business and eager to please Dad. Matthew was the free spirit, the "baby" of the family, of whom little was expected. Their college choices reflected their personalities; Harley earned a degree in Finance from Ohio State, and Matthew studied Drama and Communications at the University of New Orleans.

Both sons joined the business immediately on graduating from college. Harley conscientiously applied himself to his role as "president-trainee" though Wes did little directly to prepare Harley as his eventual successor. Matthew took the job a little less seriously at first, dabbling in local theater and doing some free-lance writing.

As the Peterson Agency nears its 40th anniversary, Wes is considering some organizational changes. He and Ellie are enjoying their long weekends at their farm in Indiana, and maybe it is time to cut back his workload even further. This would, however, require loosening his grip on control of the company and he is not sure that he is ready for that, or that his sons are ready to pick up the slack.

Harley has reached a comfortable maturity with the business. His state-of-the-art finance and computing skills have provided a technical sophistication that has opened a lot of new business possibilities for the agency.

The real surprise has been Matthew; after a tentative start, he has really taken to the business. Matt earned an MBA from the University of Cincinnati, and seemed to be a natural manager. Matt began to apply his creativity to the business, and had successfully driven a diversification and growth campaign initiated by Wes.

Wes' "right-hand man" and agency general manager, Ray Duarte, could see that some change was in the works, and it made him uncomfortable. With 10 years to go before retirement, Ray knew he could not compete with Wes' sons to head the agency, and wondered how his role might change.

Wes needed a "sounding board" to explore the possibilities for scaling back his duties, while redistributing his responsibilities. Dennis

French, his CPA, knew his situation well and had advised him on a tax-favorable approach to pass company ownership to his children as part of an estate plan. It was time to expand the discussions with Dennis, and this time Wes would take Ellie along.

 **PUT YOURSELF IN THEIR SHOES**

- Is it time for Wes to name a successor? Whom should it be? Why? Is Wes ready to begin to let go of control of the company?

- Are either of Wes' sons ready to take charge? If not, what must be done to get one or both of them ready? Should there be a period with Ray in charge? If not, what is in store for Ray?

- What should the criteria for Wes' estate plan be? Is Ellie appropriately involved? Should business ownership be divided equally between their sons? How can Susan be treated equitably?

This situation, and the direction in which it is headed, illustrates many of the problems and potential problems of the family business structure:

(1)   Role of the Spouse

Ellie, despite having no active role in the business, could be a valuable business asset to Wes if he would let her. While Wes views Ellie's interest as being limited to how their financial resources will transfer to the following generation, she is probably far more in tune with the hopes, fears, and aspirations of all three children than Wes will ever be.

Family business consultant Craig Aronoff suggests that often "Mom's" role is as "Chief Emotional Officer" of the company. This is often true whether or not she is actively involved in the company.

(2)   Birth Order and Gender Issues

Many business founders view the capabilities of their children in the context of a hierarchy or "pecking order" determined at birth. Family business consultant John Curtis, of the Orlando Consulting Group offers these observations on birth order effect:

- Firstborns:
Raised as male, regardless of gender. Reared with duties, responsibilities, and expectations. Evolve into leadership roles.

- Middle:
Good kids who don't get into trouble. Never going to be first, or last. Troupers, not chiefs. Good negotiators.

- "Baby:"
Creative, rebellious, and spoiled. Not comfortable with close supervision on the job, because they didn't get it at home.

- Only:
Much like the baby. Used to getting their own way.

Misguided tradition can also cost the business the potentially valuable services of female offspring, as daughters are "programmed" to think that the business is for men only, or that raising a family and having a career are incompatible. Research published in 1993 by Mass Mutual indicates that sons are involved in the operations of 37% of family businesses, while only 16% had daughters in the business.

Even when daughters participate, they are often channeled into positions where they do not supervise men, such as human resources or customer service. These jobs are seldom viewed as preparation for the executive ranks.

How well do these generalizations fit the Petersons? How do they relate to your experience?

(3)   Reluctance of the Founder to Yield Control

The authoritative parent passes ownership of the firm gradually to the next generation, minimizing tax consequences, but fails to pass control as systematically. Wes' sons will probably have a significant share of the stock in the company well before they are taken seriously by Wes as company executives or as capable of taking the helm of the business.

Even when the "children" are in their 30s, Wes still remembers twice as many years when they were, in his view, immature and irresponsible, as there have been years when they were significant contributors to business success. Their business participation has still been largely as beginners, working under Dad's watchful eye, within the office system created by Dad and altered to his taste over 40 years.

The successor generation is almost uniformly better educated than the founder generation, more accepting of technology, and more "enlightened" about "human resources." This can be a source of considerable friction, as the Founder feels that his experience and industry knowledge are far more useful than his children's "book learning." And how dare they suggest that there might be a better way to do things?

Wes' sons, as in the case of many family businesses, have only known the business as a success; Wes still vividly remembers the struggling years, and still believes they are only one bad management decision away from returning. The business is, therefore, run very conservatively, with too much "idle" cash and too great a reluctance to take on debt.

"Successor development" is a foreign concept to Wes; let them learn from the ground up, like he did. Beginning to give them the responsibility of operating the company while Wes is still around just would not feel right. And anyway, they would probably spend and borrow "recklessly" without his firm and experienced hand.

But these concerns often mask the real reason for the Founder's reluctance to give up control. This is more than a business, it is his creation; it is in many ways the child Wes is closest to. His identity and place in the community are "wrapped around" the business. And what will he do with himself with all the time he will have on his hands?

(4)   Financial Issues

Crafting a technically optimal financial plan, that is, one which minimizes taxes, is a fairly straightforward process. A plan that provides for the financial security of the founder, recognizes the contributions of those children working in the business, and treats those not working in the business in a financially equivalent way, is much more difficult.

Is it enough for Wes to give Susan a cash amount equivalent to the book value of the stock given his sons? Is this value fairly expressed? Are the sons fairly compensated, or overpaid? Are their "perks" appropriate or lavish? Can any difference be made up to Susan in the form of a director's fee? Should Susan participate in any appreciation in business value?

These questions relate to the difficulty of determining an equivalence between liquid and income-producing assets. If Susan receives stock in the company, will she question some of her brothers' business decisions? Will she feel that her profit-sharing income is unfairly determined because they are paying personal expenses with business funds?

Can the business afford to pay Dad a "consulting" fee so that he can retain his standard of living as his duties are reduced? Is there enough cash in the company to buy him out, and let him live off other invest-ments?

(5)   Preferential Treatment of Family Members

Family members are generally treated, or at least perceived as being treated, preferentially over non-related associates. They are frequently hired whether there is a job opening to fill or not, regardless of qualifications or lack thereof, and are generally "fire-proof" even when they act as though they are above company rules. Their compensation is often disproportionate to their contribution.

This would seem to cause resentment among non-family employees, and usually does. Key employees are difficult to motivate when they find themselves reporting to less qualified family members; this often drives home the realization that their potential for advancement in the firm is limited. Some move on, others simply stay on while reducing their commitment.

Frequently the stresses caused by combining family and business turn out to be fatal. FORTUNE magazine (Paré, 1990) estimates that fewer than one-third of family firms "survive squabble-free into the second-generation." Even more often, the inherent complications of this combination cause the business to be less than it could be.

After a brief discussion of how the family and business interact, we will expand on these issues and suggest some approaches to addressing them.

The Family/Business System

(1)   Inherent Conflicts

The family business must be thought of as a system, consisting of family, business and ownership, with varying degrees of overlap. Members of the family may or may not own stock, may or may not work in the business; frequently a family member with partial owner-ship is not active in the management of the business

This creates widely differing objectives among the participants in the system. Those not active in the business view it as merely an income stream, and may resent the lessening of that stream by what they perceive as excessive compensation and perquisites for the active members. Active members may resent drawing out dividends for the inactive members rather than re-investing those funds in the business. Even within the actives, many perceive rewards to be unrelated to contribution to the business.

An individual within the family business system is inseparable from the family network of relationships; it is unnatural for a person to discipline his or her parent, aunt or uncle in the business environment. The emotional processes of that network must be respected, though they are often not in the best interests of the business. The system is often precariously balanced by recognition of things better left unsaid, and people better worked around.

Real Scenario 11:   The Peterson Agency - Ownership Distribution

Wes decided to split ownership equally among his three chil-dren. His CPA's recommendation for fair treatment rules was as follows:

- Salaries:
  Harley and Matthew would set their compensation package.
  The CPA would compare it to norms for agencies of similar
  size; should it be excessive, the company would make up the
  difference to Susan as a Director's fee. Wes would draw a consulting fee for life of as much as he needed to maintain his lifestyle.

- Benefits:
  Susan and Wes would receive all company benefits as Directors.

- Risk:
  Wes would have veto power over all major commitments of
  company funds recommended by Harley and/or Matthew.
  Should Harley and Matthew split on a major decision, then
  Susan would vote her shares as a tiebreaker.

- Future:
  Susan's children would have equal access to business employment with Harley's and Matthew's.

PUT YOURSELF IN THEIR SHOES

- Is there any legal problem with the rules? Any ethical problem?

- Do the rules insure fair treatment of all parties? Are they complete? Do you see any problems in implementation?

- What assumptions are required by these rules? About business
  success? About profits?

- Should Harley and Matthew make the same salary, no matter what their responsibilities? Will Wes' open-ended compensation program cause any problems?

- What will happen if Susan is forced to break a tie, essentially siding with one brother over the other on a major business initiative? Will she know enough about the business to genuinely contribute to the decision? What other criteria might she use; the brother she likes better, the more aggressive one, the one with the more convincing reasons, etc.?

(2) The Family Business Environment

Some assumptions can be made about the environment in which the family business operates. Each family has a culture, or set of values, that family members accept without question, often without even realizing. Information seen as inconsistent with family beliefs, or somehow a threat to relationships vital to the family culture, is often rejected no matter how compelling.

A far greater premium is generally placed on the avoidance of conflict than in non-family firms. Old ways of solving problems, known to avoid offending family sensitivities, are continually applied whether or not they are appropriate. Some problems are not even addressed, where probable solutions would disturb family equilibrium. Business systems and accountability are often very informal within the family firm, as members assume roles they are not yet ready for, and often receive titles and compensation that greatly exceed ability.

Real Scenario 11:   The Peterson Agency - Control Distribution

While Wes was satisfied that he had "solved" the problem of passing company ownership to the next generation, distributing the control that he was willing to relinquish presented a stickier issue. Harley was highly competent technically, but had a narrow perspective on the business and seemed to have little business "sense." Matt had a wider business perspective, was more creative and better with people, but a bit irresponsible and highly distracted by his other interests.

Wes knew he had to make some title changes at the top; there was enough skepticism already about whether he was really beginning to cut back his involvement. He considered naming Ray president for a few years while seasoning his sons a bit more, but decided that the company needed more dynamic leadership than Ray could provide.

The Peterson family dynamic would drive this decision as it did most personal and business decisions. Wes would not consult or discuss, but assume that he knew what Ellie thought, and the "boys'" preferences. He would develop a plan in his head, and begin to "program" the others to accept his approach as the only logical one. As he began to "leak" the details of his plan to the rest of the family, they might express a preference for a different approach but Wes could tactfully acknowledge their opinion without giving it any credence. This expression by the family member would be made tentatively, and dropped as soon as it became apparent that Wes' way would prevail.

In this case, the decision was that Harley would be made president, with Matt made vice-president for administration. Ray would be sales manager. Wes would suggest that Harley develop a broader view of their industry, attending trade shows and seminars given by their professional organization. Matt would be encouraged to further develop his management skills, and to take charge of their record-keeping, billing, and other administrative systems. Wes was comfortable with this plan, and prepared to be oblivious to any criticism of it. It was now time to start dropping hints of it to the beneficiaries of his wisdom.

TIME OUT! - YOUR COACH SAYS

1. Is Wes' plan a good one? Could any other final result be expected by the others? Might it have turned out any differently if Wes had openmindedly sought other opinions?

2. Whether or not you approve of Wes' approach, do you feel it is the best way to avoid conflict and bad feelings? Might a candid discussion by the entire family have been constructive in this instance? Suggest two alternatives to this solution.

Making the Most of the Family Business Structure

Keys to Keeping The Family Business Healthy

- Sources of conflict must be addressed in the most objective and constructive way possible.

- Rules for the entry of family members into the business can preempt many problems related to role and compensation. Some particularly useful requirements to consider would be whether summer or part-time work is required during school, and whether there should be a particular educational requirement (college degree, specific field). Many firms require that the family member work first for another company, often for up to 5 years.
  In practice, once a family member makes a choice of college major that is not relevant to the business, should they be excluded from joining the family firm? Can it be made up? What should be considered to meet the experience requirement? Work during school years? Work between high school and college? Military service? Volunteer activities? What if the experience requirement is not met, and the family member cannot find another job?

- Performance rules must be compatible with those of non-family employees. There must be a specific job opening for the family member, and he or she must be qualified to fill it. Compensation must be related to responsibility. Additional rewards for being a family member must be given in other ways, or with personal rather than business funds.

- A shared vision of the company must be created within the family. Items to be determined should include a common understanding of the nature of the business, and its directions. Consensus should be reached on attitudes toward growth and risk, guiding principles of how business should be conducted, and objectives for family participation and ownership.

- A mechanism to implement that vision must be designed. This requires effective communication systems, which could employ formal family meetings or a family council. Vital to that mechanism is the development, maintenance and update of guiding plans: the business/strategic plan; the transfer of control/succession plan, and the transfer of ownership/financial plan.

TIME OUT! – YOUR COACH SAYS

1. Did the Person agency have any entry rules in place?
2. Are the performance expectations for Harley and Matt differently than that of non-family members?
3. Does this organisation have a shared vision in place? What are their goals based on?
4. What is missing here and what would you do next?

Succession Planning

Succession planning begins by considering issues relative to continuity. How are succession decisions to be made, and by whom? Should the business be sold rather than continued? Will an interim, non-family, manager be needed until the successor generation is ready?

Should it be decided to continue the business, the method and timing of the transfer of control must be planned. A successor must be identified, and the grooming process begun. The current leader must be phased out in an orderly manner, and his or her financial security must be assured.

Ownership must likewise be transferred, in a manner that minimizes the tax burden. Family members must be given fair, if not identical, financial treatment. Enough liquidity must be provided to insure cash requirements can be met.

Real Scenario 11:   The Peterson Agency - Re-thinking the Succession Plan

Wes didn't know why he was having trouble in beginning to drop hints about the succession plan he had worked out in his head. There certainly was cause for anxiety on his part; the company was functioning well, and this would certainly upset the delicate balance of egos and abilities.

Ray, his most capable employee, had the misfortune of not being a Peterson. His loyalty was to Wes, and Wes did not know his attitude toward working for Wes' sons.

Harley, Wes' soon to be designated successor, should be most satisfied with the new arrangement, but he often gave the impression that he would just as soon spend his days crunching numbers on the computer and leave the bothers of management to others. As uncertain as Wes was about their responses to the plan, he drew a total blank on Matt. Did Matt want to be president? Did he think he deserved it?

Wes decided he had best get some objective feedback on his plan before unveiling it. His friend Bob Keller was in a similar business, and was well into a transition plan of his own. Bob knew a fair amount about his business, and knew the major players. Bob had worked with a family business consultant on his plan, and recommended that Wes do the same. This was all new to Wes, who prided himself on his self-sufficiency. Picking Bob's brain led to a rough outline of a plan; Wes would begin to implement it, but agreed to seek an expert if implementation stalled.

The significant elements of the plan were: Wes would form a family council to set the objectives for the transition; the first meeting would begin to develop their shared vision for the business; once there was some consensus on this vision, they would tackle the sensitive issues related to its implementation, primarily the title and responsibility structure. This was about as far out as Wes could project before seeing how these sessions went.

Wes was still not comfortable with the shared vision concept. He was still basically an insurance man, whereas his sons were much more excited about the financial planning aspects of the business, and the many new investment products coming on the market. In addition, his sons were much more willing to spend money on office appearance, computer equipment, and professional training programs. He worried that loosening his grip on the business could lead to their leading the business away from what had made it successful.

 **PUT YOURSELF IN THEIR SHOES**

- Was it a good idea for Wes to re-open consideration of his succession plan? Was it really a plan, or the default option? Was Bob a good choice to "bounce it off?" What do you think of Bob's advice?

- Is Wes' idea of starting without a consultant's guidance a good one? What are the risks? How would you assess the chances of success of this approach?

- Is Wes sufficiently committed to this participative approach to planning? Does he have a company vision to present, or is the process truly working from a "blank slate?" Does Wes value the others' opinions enough for the process to work?

- Who should be on the family council? Who should chair it? What should the rules of order be? How should conflicts be resolved? Are the goals too ambitious?

It should go without saying, but it does not, that all of the founder's children should be given fair and objective consideration as potential successors. This process is often sabotaged, as oldest sons are often led to believe that taking over the business is their birthright. Similarly, younger sons generally join the company with the understanding that they are not candidates for the top job.

According to researcher Alanna Galiano, enlightened family businesses conduct a gender and birth order "blind" succession process incorporating six strategic phases:

1. Personal development phase

In the personal development phase, successor candidates should be encouraged to work outside the family firm. This will enable them to gain real-world experience, assess their own market value, and to build self-esteem. Also, in this phase, successor candidates should seek methods for addressing the weaknesses in their family business.

2. Mentorship

Once the candidates enter the family firm, the founder should select a mentor for each. A mentor can provide leadership guidance, teaching the successor candidates about the company's history and culture and other aspects of the business. Required performance evaluations will enable the mentor to coach the successor candidates on areas deserving of attention in their development programs. It is preferable that this mentor not be a family member.

3. Selection of a successor

When it comes time to select a successor, family member or not, the founder must establish a set of objective criteria on which to base the decision. To aid in this objectivity, the founder may wish to consult with an outside board of advisors, non-family executives in other companies, or may attempt to develop a family consensus. If no family member is quite ready, naming an interim non-family leader should be considered.

4. Training for leadership

The designated successor should receive formal leadership skills training necessary to assume control of the firm. Next, the successor should receive the opportunity to operate a visible department within the firm as a trial run. During this phase, the mentors are still important. Often, successors may go through a period when they reassess their commitment to the firm and they may lose focus as they try to establish their identity as leaders distinct from the founder. Mentors should communicate that the path is not predetermined for the successor, that he or she must create it. To find support during this transition, many successors join peer groups to associate and share experiences with other successors in family firms.

5. The founder's new role must slowly evolve

Throughout the leadership development process, the founder's new role should evolve. In this phase, the successor should gradually assume new responsibilities from the founder, keeping in mind an ultimate transfer date. When owners establish this deadline, they must commit to surrendering control of the firm to the successor, without the possibility that the founder might later re-assume control. Founders without outside interests have the most difficulty relinquishing control. Often, founders who grapple with leaving are given an "emeritus" status as a member of the firm for life.

6. The importance of communication in the succession process

To ensure a smooth transition, the founder should communicate clearly to family and non-family members that a successor has been chosen through a planned selection process based on objective criteria. Once all founder responsibilities are transferred, organizational succession is complete, thereby leaving the firm on a path for family continuity.

Real Scenario 11:   The Peterson Agency - Family Council

When Wes suggested formation of the Council to discuss the future of the business, an unspoken "what is he up to?" ran through the others' minds. Ellie and Susan were surprised, and pleased, that they were asked to participate.

Wes, as interim chairman, called the first Family Council meeting to order. After setting the agenda, they would discuss how the chairmanship would be assigned from then on. Wes was almost sidetracked by a swelling up of pride in his family, what a fine group of people they were, and their level of mutual support. But there was work to be done, and maybe it would not be so hard after all.

The first item to be discussed was each "child's" view of the future of the business and their role in that future. Susan expressed a far greater interest and pride in the business than anyone but Ellie knew she had. The boys had the greatest respect for her knowledge and judgment, and asked that her board membership become real and engaged rather than merely a vehicle for paying her.

Harley suggested that he prepare a strategic plan for the post-Wes Peterson Agency, with the others' input. and present it to the Council the following month. He roughed out his plans and priorities for the business in a reasoned and self-assured manner he had seldom exhibited in the past.

Matt's vision was more aggressive than Harley's, as he proposed expansion into other cities with a catalog of financial products and computer linkages. He volunteered that he would concede the presidency of the company to Harley, but would like to be in charge of the branch network.

Ellie proposed that Susan draw up entry rules for the next generation's entering the business, and chair future Council meetings. Her motions passed by acclamation.

Wes was thoroughly pleased by the developing meeting of the minds. His kids had come a whole lot further than he gave them credit for. He felt regrets for not having confided in Ellie sooner.

Wes suggested that his assignment for the next meeting be to shop for a tractor and other equipment to get that farm into shape, and handed the imaginary gavel over to Susan.

 **PUT YOURSELF IN THEIR SHOES**

- Is this a likely scenario? Where does it depart from expectations? What might a likelier outcome have been?

- Assuming it did happen this way, could everyone have been on their best behavior this time with the fireworks to come later? Where are the potential breakdowns in harmony?

- Can Wes let this process proceed without becoming more directive? Where is it most likely to get out of his comfort range?

- From this beginning, how would you rate the chances of the process yielding a consensus plan that everyone can live with? What are the major obstacles?

TIME OUT! - YOUR COACH SAYS

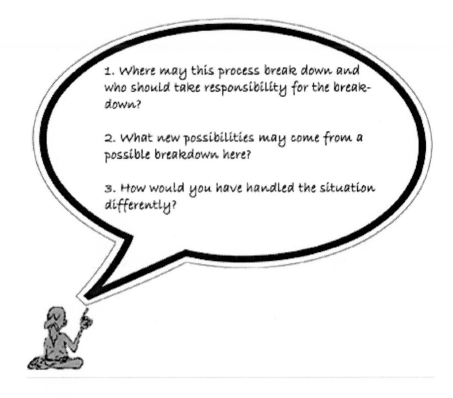

1. Where may this process break down and who should take responsibility for the break-down?

2. What new possibilities may come from a possible breakdown here?

3. How would you have handled the situation differently?

Summary

Family firms have all the concerns and challenges of other businesses, compounded and complicated by additional issues unique to a family business structure. These issues include the role of the spouse, birth order and gender of the successor generation, reluctance of the founder to yield control, financial equity between family members, and motivation of non-family employees.

Successful family businesses "take care of business." They maintain their professionalism and objectivity, often by involving and conferring with consultants and/or outside board members. They cultivate the spirit of enterprise and review their attitude toward risk as opportunities emerge. Their collective eye is on the future, with programs for successor identification and development, and the policy that retirement is irrevocable.

They are flexible about disinvestment by family owners not involved in the business ("pruning the family tree"). They honor non-family employees by compensation plans that recognize contribution to success, and by being sensitive enough to understate wealth and privileges, if appropriate. They maintain and refine their shared vision of the business. They educate and involve inactive family owners and in-laws in the business, its successes and challenges. They adapt family participation policies to changing abilities and interests.

Most of all, successful family businesses cherish the family. They accept their individual differences, and deal with conflict immediately and constructively. They maintain their commitment to family precepts and values, keep their long-term perspective, and continue to enjoy each other's company.

Real Scenario 12: Tammany Supply, Inc. (E)

After several difficult years, Tammany Supply, Inc. (TSI) seemed finally to be back on solid footing in mid-1992. The 1990 to 1992 Business Plan for the Covington, LA plumbing wholesaler (see the "D" case) had turned out to be conservative. Sales for 1990 exceeded those of 1989 by almost 20 percent; while 1991 was essentially standstill, 1992 would apparently show another 20% sales growth and the best profit performance in 5 years.

Company president John Vinturella had spent the previous year in a three-quarter time academic position in New Orleans, which left only one day a week free to spend at the business. He was finding himself increasingly detached from the business on this schedule. While keeping a firm grip on the policy-making function, John could sense some slippage in operations. He felt he needed one more stable, mature hand to assist general manager Ron Stewart in guiding the company's return to health and beyond.

RETURN TO FAMILY BUSINESS

TSI had not operated as a family business since spinning off from the company owned by John's father and brothers (see the "A" case). Vinturella's now grown children had each spent some time in TSI, but had shown no interest in making it a career. Both earned advanced degrees; Vicki is a lawyer, and David is involved in sports promotion in Atlanta.

In the fall of 1992, John offered a position in the company to Vicki's husband, Scott Olson. Scott had just graduated from college, was an Army veteran, having seen service in Europe, and had worked full-time for several years, even while taking a heavy college course load. In addition, he was the father of a new baby (John's first grandchild).

John's recruiting pitch would not have won any salesmanship awards. Scott would report to Ron, and should not expect John to intervene or provide for any special treatment. Scott would be paid an amount commensurate with his duties; "perks" of ownership would come in due time. The hours would be long, and much of the work would be tedious. How could Scott say no to such a job description?

Scott joined TSI in August, 1992. John convinced himself that he was not creating a job for Scott, that he needed an assistant general manager for operations. Convincing himself that Scott was qualified was a bit more of a stretch; Scott's degree was in Geography and he had no applicable work experience. As John examined his motives, he tried to weigh the importance of the comfort of having a son-in-law as Ron's right-hand man, and his daughter involved in the details of the business, if only indirectly.

NATURE OF THE BUSINESS

A case could be made that the major qualifications for the AGM position were a college degree and some maturity; the nuts-and-bolts of the industry could be learned fairly quickly. While the degree might seem an odd basic requirement, John felt that it was a key to growth potential, and no one below Ron had a degree. In addition, Scott was 28 years old and had a very good work ethic.

The advancement path in this type of business was that every one started as a truck driver, generally fresh out of high school. The better truck drivers became warehousemen; the others stayed as truck drivers, or moved on. The more intelligent and personable warehousemen became inside salesmen; The more organized and capable inside salespersons took on administrative duties, such as purchasing and pricing, and generally "topped out" there.

The exceptions to this path were the "skill" positions. Ron was hired as credit manager, Anna as showroom manager and chief administrator. Bill was hired at startup as an outside salesman, and had evolved into an all-purpose mentor, trainer, and customer service consultant.

John was concerned about the next generation of leadership for TSI. Bill and Anna were near retirement, portending a significant decrease in the experience level of the company. Of the senior salespersons, Keith, 30 years old, was the technical person with a firm grip on purchasing and pricing; Kevin, 25, was the best sales person TSI ever had.

But where would the initiative come from? Ron did not have an owner's perspective, and was taking on an increasing administrative burden. As John's involvement lessened, who would take on his financial duties, and his role as management analyst and quality controller?

THE SUCCESSION PROCESS BEGINS

There are a few "givens" in this case that constrain any transition plan for TSI.

First of all, it is time for a transition plan. John has separated himself from the day-to-day operation of the business, and this separation seems to be irreversible. He maintains a quality control interest, but it is getting to be less and less detailed. While his approval would be required for any major policy changes, he cannot be expected to initiate any. Other factors contribute to the sense of transition time. The company is about to suffer a significant decrease in experience level. A family member of the successor generation is entering.

Secondly, there will need to be some period during which Ron is in charge. Ron has been a very effective GM, and has every right to expect to be "acting" president as John detaches more and more. Scott is certainly years away from being able to take over, and any attempt to rush the process would be very disturbing to a system that is functioning very well.

Finally, there is little doubt in anyone's mind that Scott will be the next "real" president of the company. Ron is neither a family member nor an owner; he is a responsible, dedicated, effective employee, but "family member" will outrank that almost every time.

THE DILEMMA OF THE KEY NON-FAMILY EMPLOYEE

Ron is a victim of a cruel reality of family business: a merely adequate family member will almost always pass up an outstanding non-family member on the advancement ladder. At this point, Scott is an unknown; he could turn out to be better than Ron, or he could be a total disaster.

When John began to separate from the business, he appointed Ron GM over Bill and Anna because Ron was easily the best manager of the three. Ron responded well to the recognition of his performance, and to his increasing empowerment in personnel and financial matters. John was impressed by the clarity of Ron's judgment relative to what should be cleared with John, and what he should handle directly.

Over the past two years, the transfer of duties from John to Ron had gotten well under way. Ron was beginning to achieve a sense of quasi-ownership, taking over the signing of checks, representing the company in a wide range of activities, getting significantly larger bonuses than other employees, and receiving other miscellaneous perquisites of the position.

John's first personnel decision in two years was to hire Scott, and Ron was not consulted. Before Scott began, John described to Ron his perception of Scott's role as Ron's assistant; Scott would take over many of Ron's administrative duties, and would supervise the warehouse and delivery operation. Ron was expected to groom Scott as his replacement, but that replacement would not take place for ten years, until Ron was within two years of retirement. Ron seemed comfortable with these conditions, and the transition was on.

THE SUCCESSOR DEVELOPMENT PROGRAM

While John's discussion with Ron emphasized Scott's subordinate role, the first post-employment discussion with Scott emphasized the exciting possibilities of that role. In his attempt at making sure Scott understood the downside of the position, John was almost discouraging Scott from joining; now that Scott was part of the team, John had to shift into a motivational mode.

He first counseled patience; Scott's development program was going to take 10 years, 5 years of increasing knowledge and ability, followed by 5 years of developing responsibility and judgment. In the first phase Scott would have to work harder than anyone else there, to achieve the credibility he would need for phase 2. Phase 2 would be more enjoyable, as his fellow employees recognize his successor-designate status, hopefully considering it earned rather than inherited.

Some specific objectives for Scott in phase 1 were: to become TSI's most knowledgeable person on the company software; to become the TSI management analyst (cash flow, general ledger, monitoring TSI performance against industry norms, tracking inventory utilization), and; to continually improve product knowledge, and supervisory and customer service skills (through self-study and/or formal seminars).

THE FIRST BIG STEP IS A STUMBLE

John started Scott as operations manager, supervising fairly junior employees (truck drivers and warehousemen), and scheduling deliveries to maximize customer service. Bill had been doing this as part of his too-many duties, and some slippage was occurring. Scott could sharpen operations, impressing the senior employees and getting some sense of tangible accomplishment. Wrong! Bill resented the loss of his supervisory duties, the operations staff resisted taking orders from someone who knew so little about the product line, and Kevin felt that Scott had "leapfrogged" him on the advancement ladder.

John had caused the problem, and it was up to him to fix it. He told Bill that it was time to make way for the younger generation, and put Bill in charge of inside sales and training; while not entirely satisfied, Bill saved some face and saw the handwriting on the wall. TSI's best truck driver, Dan, was elevated to operations supervisor, giving orders under Scott's direction; he was in enough over his head to appreciate Scott's assistance.

Kevin, as a key member of the next generation of leadership, posed a more difficult situation; John reminded Kevin that he had shown no interest in Scott's position, and that Kevin's input to operations, as their primary "customer," was vital. He was asked to understand that Scott's college degree would be as useful to the company in the long run as Kevin's 4 years of experience.

John felt as though they had recovered from the mis-step, and that no real harm was done. He realized though that, for a time, he would have to raise his level of awareness of the company management "dynamic," until Scott was better accepted.

PUT YOURSELF IN THEIR SHOES

- What do you think of John's timing in bringing Scott into the business? Was there really a position available, or was it rationalized? Should other candidates have been considered before turning to Scott? What additional did Scott bring to the business due to being a family member? Was John meeting his needs at the expense of the business?

- What was John's purpose in initially describing the position to Scott so negatively? Did Scott take it as negatively as presented, or discount it some? What do you think is his motivation to take the position? Is it a good fit?

- What effect will Scott's position have on Ron's motivation? Should John have given Ron "veto power" over the hire? Does Ron accept John's transition timetable, or suspect the change will happen sooner? How would Ron view John's choice of Scott's duties?

- Is Scott's development plan consistent with what John told Ron? Is it too ambitious? Is this merely a "menu," to be revised to include only those tasks at which Scott shows he can do well? Is John being too directive; should he let Scott's duties evolve more?

- Was any permanent harm done by the problems with Scott's initial assignment? If so, how will this harm manifest itself? Is Scott or John viewed as the culprit? Were the accommodating changes appropriate? Will they work in the longer-term? How will this affect the relationships between John, Ron and Scott?

TIME OUT! - YOUR COACH SAYS

1. Where may this process break down and who should take responsibility for the breakdown?

2. What new possibilities may come from a possible breakdown here?

3. How would you have handled the situation differently?

Chapter 7
Small Business Management

Beyond Startup

In a classic Harvard Business Review article, Neil Churchill and Virginia Lewis identify and describe what they refer to as "The five stages of small business growth."

Until now, we have focused primarily on Stage 1, or what they term as "Existence." This stage is characterized by acquiring customers and delivering satisfactory products and/or services in sufficient quantity to become a viable business.

Stage 2, after having demonstrated some market acceptance, may be considered "Survival." In this stage, we may consider our primary challenge to be generating enough cash flow to stay in business and finance growth to achieve an economic return on our capital and efforts. We will discuss cash flow and progress measurement in the following section.

Stage 3 is when we may consider ourselves a "Success." Success is actually less a stage than a plateau; it also represents a significant crossroads. Many business owners use this plateau as a launching pad for growth, passing through a **Stage 4:** "Take-Off" to **Stage 5:** "Resource Maturity."

Other successful business owners choose to enjoy life on the plateau. Churchill and Lewis refer to this as "Disengagement," characterized by the owner passing responsibilities on to professional staff members. The business then generally takes on a defensive posture, holding its position rather than exploring any new frontiers. We will discuss disengagement in the final section of this chapter.

Before proceeding to the stages after "existence," however, we will briefly discuss a prerequisite for a successful business, namely a commitment to ethical behavior, community involvement, and social responsibility. The first tests of our business ethics may occur while working for others, but these tests become more difficult as we consider, and then pursue entrepreneurial opportunities.

(1)   The Ethical Individual

It should go without saying that the ethical individual does not steal from or lie to an employer or a customer; these are the easy situations in which to determine ethical behavior. But what about all the little opportunities to shade the truth, or leave out an important detail, or make unauthorized use of company resources, or pad an expense account; where does salesmanship or discretion end, and unethical behavior begin?

The person working for someone else while considering starting a new venture can also encounter some difficult ethical dilemmas. How long can the prospective entrepreneur work for a firm while planning to start up a competitor? What actions within that role are permissible, and which could be considered advancing their personal cause at their firm's expense?

For the startup entrepreneur, the temptations are great to over-represent assets and understate liabilities. Most are strapped for resources, and fear the unvarnished truth may not be sufficient to get the needed resource commitments.

(2)   The Ethical Company

Businesses operate with the presumption of trustworthiness. Those that violate that trust soon run out of one-time victims. Long-term success is built on lasting relationships, which depend on kept promises and fair treatment.

It is not a wishful or idealistic observation to say that a company does well by doing good. Highly ethical companies earn the trust of their customers and other strategic partners, and this leads to mutually beneficial relationships. Employees are proud to work for companies that treat them with respect, and their performance reflects it.

But there is more to ethical behavior than honesty and consideration. A broader term that reflects a proactive component is social responsibility. Companies that invest in their communities are rewarded many times over. Internships and summer jobs for local students, sponsorship of community organizations, and participation in food banks and charity drives are all ways to strengthen our bonds to the community while giving us a justifiably great feeling about our company.

Little good comes to us that is not a return on some investment we have made. There are few professional rewards as great as the feeling of being a contributing member of the community, and of the extended family that we and our associates can become.

Real Scenario 13:   How could that be an ethical problem?

Sherry Blaylock was ahead of her time when she started Net Profits, Inc., a consulting firm for businesses considering an Internet presence, but it is beginning to pay off in the spring of 1996. Carol Harvey signed on in the early days, and now heads a sales force of 6 people while Sherry concentrates on the creative side of the business.

Carol has decided that she really wants to start a similar business of her own, and has been developing a business plan for her new company on her own time. She continues to do her job well, and does not plan to tell Sherry about her new venture until she is ready to give notice.

Carol is finding that her situation is beginning to create some tough ethical questions for her. She would like to take one of her salespersons, Bill Blake, with her to the new company. Several of her current clients with NPI would come over to the new venture; asking for commitments from them now would significantly ease her attempts at raising startup funds. How much farther can she go while drawing a paycheck from NPI?

 **PUT YOURSELF IN THEIR SHOES**

- Is it possible for Carol to be giving her best to NPI in her current frame of mind? Should she continue with NPI once she begins to develop a business plan? Once she has decided that she will probably start her own firm? Once she is definite?

- Can she ethically discuss her plans with Bill Blake now? Can she begin to negotiate terms of employment with him?

- Should she approach her current customers for a written commitment to doing business with her new company to present to her banker in confidence? How would you expect her customers to react? How would her banker view such letters?

TIME OUT! - YOUR COACH SAYS

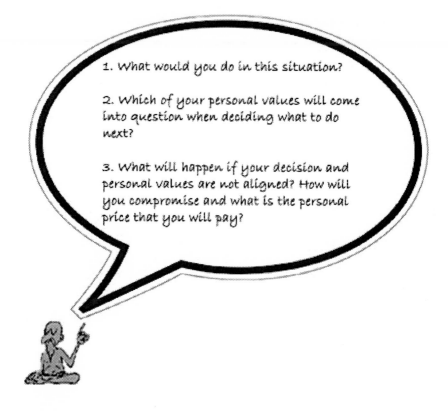

The Survival Stage

Cash Flow and Performance Measurement

The amount of time required for a new venture to reach profitability is a critical factor in whether or not a business survives the startup trauma. A promising new business, well on its way to viability, can still experience severe cash flow problems; sometimes these can be fatal. Even beyond the startup period, strains on cash can severely limit company growth.

Most managers know what the income statement tells them, but few manage the balance sheet as well. In particular, proper cash management permits the owner to meet the cash needs of the business, take advantage of special buys and discounts, minimize interest expense, and ride out slow periods. A good cash position allows the owner to maintain an adequate level of inventory, replace equipment as needs arise, and to seize expansion opportunities.

Cash demands are often cyclical. On an annual cycle, inventory can be worked down (in essence, partially liquidated) as a slow period approaches, and restocked as the prime selling season returns. On a monthly cycle, a manager can create inducements for customers to pay in time to fill in "troughs" in the cash balance.

For many businesses, the primary management control on cash is collecting on accounts receivable. Are you in the lending business? Do you mean to be? Carefully screen credit applicants; require a signed application that spells out credit terms. Take immediate action on past-due accounts, and earn a reputation for pursuing defaulters and bad-check artists. Do not be reluctant to cut off those who are beginning to owe you more than they are worth.

Another control is accounts payable management; negotiate extended credit terms where possible, but do not abuse your vendors. Pay promptly when the cash is there, and ask their help when it is not. Other balance sheet items can offer opportunities to improve your cash position. Do you have an "edifice complex?" Has your physical plant exceeded what is business-necessary? Show an expense conscious-ness, and the attitude will spread to your employees. Clear out dead and excess inventory; there is a cost to carrying it.

Is there a point at which a company's cash position can become too strong? Maintaining a cash balance that far exceeds a comfortable operating cushion in a non-interest-bearing account will certainly drag down the rate of return on our investment. Short and intermediate term excess could be invested temporarily in interest-bearing instru-ments that can quickly be converted to cash. Longer term excess can require a strategic reevaluation, to consider expansion, diversification, paying down debt, or a huge bonus to the owner.

How can we measure a company's performance relative to these guidelines? While the financial statements give us values for many of the parameters we use as management controls, some relative measures can be even more meaningful. These measures are often expressed as ratios of standard financial statement items. There are several widely used ratios that allow us to compare our performance to norms for our industry.

Real Scenario 13:   So, how are we doing so far?

The tax return for Tammany Supply, Inc. for 1994 is complete, and TSI President John Vinturella has decided that it is time to look at some company performance measures. He has routinely calculated some basic percentages, but would like to delve a little deeper this time.

The first two columns of the table below show summaries of the company's Income Statement and Balance Sheet, with some of the key management control variables set off in gray. John would prefer to have a higher gross margin, but the observed 18.7% is satisfactory given their aggressive sales effort; for the past 3 years TSI has posted sales increases over the previous year of 20%+.

The net margin is acceptable, near industry norms published by the American Supply Association, while returns on investment and equity comfortably exceed norms. Collection days, or average days from invoicing to collection, are 20% better (i.e. less) than is typical for similar businesses.

The third column represents financial ratios that TSI's accountant suggests that John track. John has calculated the ratios, and we will help him to interpret them following this case. Dun and Bradstreet norms for home supply businesses will add some perspective to our consideration.

Tammany Supply Inc. 1994

Income:		Expenses:	
Sales	$4,362,904	Personnel	$379,544
Cost of Goods sold	$3,545,747	Operations	$174,857
Gross Mrgin	18.7%	Sales	$51,561
Other Income	$10,813	Administration	$98,739
Total Income	$827,970	Depreciation	$29,296
		Total Expenses	$733,996
		Profit/Loss BIT	$93,974
		Taxes	$20,201
		Profit/Loss after taxes	$73,773
		Net Margin	1.96%
		Return on Investment	6.63%

TIME OUT! - YOUR COACH SAYS

1. How applicable are industry norms to a specific small business? Are differences from norms more reflective of quality of management, operating strategies, or competitive conditions?

2. Is rapid increase in sales volume a valid reason for a low gross margin? Does an acceptable net margin validate this approach?

3. Does a return on equity of about 10% represent an effective use of our personal resources?

Assets:				1994 Ratios:	1994 TSI	D&B Norms
Cash	$101,407		Liquidity/Indebtedness			
Accounts Receivable	$430,486	1	Cur Assets/Cur Debt	2.62	2.24
Collection Days	36.01	2	"Acid Test"	1.77	
Inventory	$326,554	3	TotLiab/TotAssets	34.53	
OthCur Assets	$148,312	4	CurDebt/TangNetWor	52.0	75.0
Total Current Assets	$1,006,759	5	TotDebt/TangNetWor	52.0	124.7
Total Fixed Assets	$105,713	6	CurDebt/Inventory	117.6	81.2
Total Assets	$1,112,472				
			Sales/Profitability		
Liabilities:		7	NetSales/TangNetWor	5.91	3.84
Accounts Payable	$356,320	8	NetSales/NetWkCap	7.01	5.39
OthCur Liabilities	$27,777	9	NetSales/Inventory	13.4	4.5
Net Working Capital	$728,375	10	NetProf/NetSales	1.69	1.58
Long-Term Debt	$0	11	NetProf/TangNetWor	9.99	7.29
Total Liabilities	$384,097	12	NetProf/NetWkCap	11.85	8.66
Equity	$738,375		Other Normed		
Return on Equity	9.99%	13	FxAssets/TangNetWor	14.3	32.8
Total Liab/Eq	$1,122,472	14	Inventory/NetWkCap	44.8	93.3

The following discussion of financial ratios references the table in the previous case.

(1) Liquidity and Indebtedness (Indicators of financial stability and leverage)

The liquidity of a firm indicates its ability to meet cash requirements, ride out difficult times, and expand in good times. Ratio 1, current assets to current liabilities, is a widely used measure of liquidity referred to as the current ratio. Ratio 2, the "acid-test" is thought to be a better measure because it uses current assets less inventory (generally our least liquid current asset). Ratio 3 shows total liabilities to be less than 35% of total assets. Based on norms, TSI seems to be comparatively liquid. What would illiquidity convey? What are ways of improving liquidity?

Another measure of the financial stability of a firm is its use of indebtedness, sometimes referred to as its financial leverage. Ratio 4 shows current debt as 52% of tangible net worth, or equity. Ratio 5 shows total debt to equity the same as current, since there is no long-term debt. Ratio 6, current debt to inventory, is high relative to norms. Is this inconsistent with the previous ratios? Do we need more information? Is this more of an indicator of TSI's rapid inventory turnover?

The comparisons to norms indicate that TSI is not very leveraged. Is this a positive or a negative? Should TSI borrow $250,000 to be more in line with norms? What might it do with the money?

(2)   Sales and Profitability (Indicators of performance)

Ratios 7 and 8 show that TSI is getting a good sales yield on its equity and its working capital. Ratio 9 is a tangible measure of its rapid inventory turnover, triple the industry norm! Combined with earlier indicators, should TSI borrow to increase its inventory? Do we know if their level of inventory is holding the business back? Should they consider a greater depth of existing inventory, or additional product lines? What market factors would determine their actions?

The profitability measures in ratios 10, 11, and 12 also comfortably exceed norms. These represent, respectively, the percentage of each sales dollar that TSI brings to the "bottom line," its return on equity, and its working capital growth rate. What do these ratios say about TSI as an investment? What types of management actions produce these results?

(3)   Analysis and Conclusions

Ratios 13 and 14 offer two more normed indicators of TSI performance. Fixed assets are a relatively low percentage of equity, indicating that investment in vehicles and equipment could reasonably be considered. Inventory is less than half the norm as a percent of working capital; this is familiar.

What does all of this tell us? Is TSI management too conservative about debt? What might happen to the positive indicators on sale and profits were they to get more leverage? Are we using the ratios properly by assuming deviation from the norm is indicative of a problem? Has John developed a strategy that provides a comfortable living while making it easy to sleep nights? Is that all bad?

Success: Going for the Growth

Many entrepreneurs' primary interest is in building a "life-style" business, that is, one which provides them a living (in varying degrees of comfort) while allowing them to do what they want to do. Other entrepreneurs want to take the business as far as it can go. Decision time comes when the business works its way through the startup trauma to achieving some degree of stability.

Every business, committed to rapid growth or not, should always have a business plan in place that is updated annually. Even if our basic business does not change, our market does, the competitive environment does, and innovation and technology create more options for the consumer.

In the annual revision of the business plan, market and environmental data must be updated, and the strategic plan revisited and frequently revised. Financial data for the year recently completed must be compared with what was projected, and future projections adjusted accordingly. Reasons for deviations must be identified and addressed.

(1)   How and where do we grow?

Strategic options in a growth situation must be identified. Can we improve market share in the current market? Should we try to sell more to current customers by widening our product line? Can we cover a broader geographic area?

Are there other channels of distribution that should be considered? Is our business concept franchisable? Should we develop a branch office network? How big can we get to be? How fast can we get there?

This process is very similar to startup; we must do rigorous market research, clearly identify the specific market we will serve, formulate a strategy that effectively seizes the perceived opportunity, and develop financial projections to measure our progress.

(2)   International Opportunities

Most small business owners think only in terms of domestic markets. International opportunities, they reason, are the province of the large corporations; "multinational company" has come to be synonymous with "huge company." Typical reactions to suggestions of evaluating international markets include: "I don't have the time to deal with all the complications;" "there are too many ways to get burned; "there are enough opportunities in the U.S. (Canada, etc.)."

Trade agreements are minimizing the complications and the dangers; Export Assistance Centers are opening around the U.S.; advances in telecommunications are shrinking distances and bringing us closer and closer to the truly global economy. Market information relative to global markets is improving in availability and timeliness.

Disengagement

For the successful business, alternative paths for the future of the firm may be considered to be the pursuit of growth, or merely "holding one's own." A case could be made for there being a middle road of accepting some evolutionary growth within the current market and product offerings.

The standing-still option is generally associated with disengagement on the part of the entrepreneur. Perhaps the everyday struggles and aggravations of the business have worn them down. Or the success they have achieved may seem sufficient, whereas its expansion does not appear satisfying. Perhaps they are simply bored of doing essentially the same thing for an extended period of time.

Frequently, what drives the disengagement process is a new focus on personal fulfillment. Many disengaged business owners seek a calmer life and greater family involvement. Many actively participate in community activities; others go back to school or lose themselves in their hobbies.

Of course, the ultimate disengagement is to shut the business down, or sell it; in the case of most family businesses, giving the reins to a successor is another option.

(1)   Is it time to go?

There comes a time in the life of every business owner when he or she begins to entertain the thought of leaving the business. There can be many reasons for deciding that it may be time to move on, but they tend to fall into one of three categories: business reasons; transitional issues, or; life-stage issues.

Business reasons for moving on are not confined to failing companies; often concern about the company's inability to grow for lack of capital, or marginal returns from the business, can lead a person to consider other options. Sometimes the return on the owner's business investment would be greater from passive instruments, such as mutual funds, with more security and less stress. If no action is taken under these circumstances, the static or marginal business can become a business at risk, and options are more limited.

Transitional issues can relate to the company's ability to compete in a business that is changing rapidly, or concern about the costs of adapting to the changes required to stay competitive in that environment. Another difficult transitional issue can be a change in the ownership structure or conflicts among owners; often the only resolution is for one or more owners to sell their stake, or to liquidate the business entirely. The loss of key personnel, or some critical skill, or general workforce unrest can lead a business owner to decide that it is easier to move on than to ride out the difficulty.

Even with all going well in the business, however, issues related to the owner's life stage can raise the issue of moving on. The small business owner is president of the company the day the business opens, with no room for promotion except to "retired." If the company reaches a growth plateau, the owner's duties can become rather monotonous, and well beneath his or her abilities.

In many cases, it simply becomes time to retire, either for reasons of age or loss of enthusiasm. In family businesses, a reluctance to move on can severely retard the development of the next generation, and under-utilize valuable management resources.

Many business owners feel uncomfortable abandoning their work ethic. Many have not adequately planned for life after work, either financially, or by the development of other interests. In family businesses, there is frequently the concern that the next generation is not up to the challenge.

(2)   Preparing to Leave the Business

There are three basic levels of planning for leaving a business: no planning needed, it will take care of itself; a one-step plan, namely sell and forget about it, and; an orderly longer-term approach. What are the risks of the two lower-level approaches?

Chances of receiving the greatest long-term return on our business investment are greatest with thoughtful advance planning. If the business is to be sold, it can be conditioned for enhanced value.

In a family business, we must determine whether there is or will be a suitable successor, possibly after a period of non-family business leadership. If so, the grooming process, transferring responsibility from leader to successor generation, should begin early enough to proceed gradually. If there is not a suitable successor on the horizon, then planning for selling the business may be the best option.

Conditioning a business for sale is similar to getting a house ready to sell. We must truthfully prepare a good case for the property's benefits for a purchaser, and present the property at its best. A professional evaluator can help us with a realistic asking price, and their experience could help them identify improvements worth making to maximize our eventual selling price.

Our sales presentation should include "recast" financial statements that make the statements more "owner-neutral". Closely-held companies often understate earnings in some way to minimize taxes; prospective buyers are more interested in maximizing profits.

Ways to improve the business' presentation include getting rid of obsolete inventory, upgrading equipment, and general housekeeping. Business appraisers can help identify other areas for improvement, and suggest a range for asking price.

(3)   Evaluating the Business

Our most effective tool in selling the business is a realistic view of what it is worth to a "stranger." This requires a dispassionate look at the "story" behind the numbers in the financial statement. This process was discussed at some length in Chapter 2 from the prospective buyer's point of view; the following checklist overlaps that material somewhat, but leans more toward the seller's perspective:

Adjusted Book Value

- Accounts Receivable:
  Allow a reasonable amount for bad and questionable debt.
- Inventory:
  Allow for obsolete, and damaged goods, and for overstock.
- Equipment:
  Deduct unusable; use replacement value for remainder.
- Accounts Payable:
  Resolve disputed amounts owed and service charges.
- Other:
  Have any business property and investments appraised
  - Recognize accruals (taxes, insurance payments, etc.)
  - Prepare payment schedules on all notes payable and receivable.
- Earnings Issues, "Goodwill"
- Salaries:
  Estimate owner-neutral compensation.
- Performance:
  Compare to lender guidelines, industry norms.
- Contracts:
  Estimate whether each adds or subtracts value.
- Personnel:
  Estimate cost to new owner if key personnel leave.
- Other:
  - Estimate value of patents, logos, and trade-marks.

Strategic Issues

Strategic issues are the least tangible, and the hardest to relate to the value of the company. Some of the questions that the owner should consider are:

- Is our market share large enough to be significant, small enough to allow growth?

- Is the competitive climate favorable to the future of the business?
- Are there any legal or technological trends impacting the future of the industry?
- Will cultural or demographic trends help or hurt future prospects?
- Can I point out growth opportunities to the new owner?
- Does my departure affect the distinctive competence of the business?

(4)   Marketing the Business

Once a thorough review of issues related to company value is conducted, we are ready to put together a sales brochure, where the business is described in general terms without being identified; this is a marketing tool for distribution and listing to attract genuine prospects.   We also need to prepare a detailed business presentation package, with background information and financial data, to give in confidence to those who express interest.

While the business presentation package has many elements in common with a business plan, its thrust is considerably different. There is no need to sell the management team, since it is essentially the management team to whom we are presenting it. Strategic possibilities may be outlined, but the chosen strategy will, of course, be determined by the new ownership.

Typical elements of the business presentation package are:

- History of the business, significant strategic changes, emerging trends.
- Company facilities and methods of operation.
- Major customers, key suppliers, and competitive climate.
- Current marketing practices, and promising possibilities.
- Evaluation of human resources available to new owners.
- Financial data and projections.

Once this information is assembled, and presented in its most salesman like manner, we can begin to prospect for buyers. A business opportunity ad in the local newspaper or business publication, or the Wall Street Journal, can quickly generate inquiries, but most will probably just be "tire kickers." Another disadvantage of this approach is that it will quickly be "on the street" that the business is for sale, and this could have a negative effect on employees and important customers.

Trade sources and associations reach a narrower but more appropriate audience, and generally can qualify prospects in a discretionary manner. These prospects will often include your competitors; while they might be serious prospects, there is some danger to advanced negotiations, as you reveal financial details and possibly a list of key customers.

Many owners offer their businesses through brokers. Larger businesses will sometimes work through merger and acquisition specialists.

Negotiations with serious prospects can focus as much on payment terms as on selling price. Be prepared to be asked to finance part of the purchase.

(5)   Passing the Business to the Next Generation

Let us briefly review the process of grooming a successor (see Chapter 5). Once the successor is chosen, the training and development process begins. Authority and responsibility is gradually shifted from the lead to the next generation. The lead generation must allow the next to use their authority, even when the lead disagrees. The most successful transitions occur on a timetable, and with a new role assigned to the lead to limit interference with the new direction the company might take.

(6)   Remaining a Productive Member of Society

The displaced owner generally has several options available once the current business is successfully sold or "handed off." Many take the resources generated, and plow them into another business or new venture. Some treat it as semi-retirement, remaining with the business in some lesser capacity, part-time or consultory.

The most "successful" retirees seem to be those who developed other interests while working, and pursue them in retirement. This could be through a "regular" job, doing something they really enjoy, with the lower stress level of employee rather than owner. Those whose financial security is assured might perform civic and volunteer activities, or catch up on their travel.

Summary

Getting the doors open on a new venture is only the first in a series of challenges on the way to entrepreneurial success. In many cases, the second (often termed "survival") stage of business development, i.e, solidifying the viability of the business, can be even more difficult.

A cornerstone of the successful long-term business is a commitment to ethical behavior, community involvement, and social responsibility. This commitment is tested while working for others, as we consider starting our own ventures, and on through the way we treat our employees. The rewards of keeping this commitment can far exceed the monetary rewards of a successful business.

Another key to business success is to carefully monitor performance, and to act on the information this process yields. Newer businesses are particularly vulnerable to problems of cash flow, as the requirements of a growing business place continual demands on today's resources. Entrepreneurs must manage the balance sheet, particularly cash and receivables, as well as the income statement, that is, the instinctive focus on sales volume. Relationships between financial statement values, in the form of ratios and percentages, can be compared to industry norms as a way of "grading" ourselves.

Once a business reaches a level of stability and prosperity that may be considered "success," the entrepreneur is at a crossroads. Many continue on a growth pattern, expanding the business in a variety of ways, sometimes even becoming international. Others become disengaged, often to the point of shutting down or selling the business.

Whatever path is chosen, the actions of the entrepreneur should always be guided by a current, well-researched, and considered business plan.

TIME OUT! - YOUR COACH SAYS

1. How can you tell which small business growth stage you are currently in?

2. What can we do to improve the cash flow of a growing business? Can cash position ever be too strong?

3. How are the commonly used financial ratios helpful in managing a business?

Real Scenario 14:   Tammany Supply, Inc. (F)

The oil price collapse of the mid-1980s took a heavy toll on the Louisiana economy.   In western St. Tammany parish, an upscale suburb of New Orleans which had been experiencing explosive growth, new residential construction fell dramatically.   For Tammany Supply, Inc. (TSI), a Covington plumbing wholesaler serving that market, sales fell 40% from 1984 to 1987.

With the assistance of a broader product line, including the opening of a patio furniture store, a modest recovery in TSI's fortunes occurred from 1988 to 1990 (see the "D" case).   Confident that the company was back on solid ground, TSI president John Vinturella began scaling back his business duties and pursuing some local academic opportunities.

By the fall of 1991, Vinturella was down to a day a week in Covington, as TSI's general manager, Ron Stewart, had risen to the occasion. In the fall of 1992, John's son-in-law, Scott Olson, joined the company and expressed interest in one day running the operation.   With Scott as Ron's right-hand man, Vinturella felt comfortable in separating even further from the business.

THE RECOVERY ACCELERATES

A building boom began in mid-1992.   TSI sales for 1992 increased 20% over 1991.   By the spring of 1993 homebuilding had become so lively that the company decided to sell its patio furniture store to an employee.   By shedding this operation, the company had undone much of the diversification it had undertaken in the late 1980s, and returned to its roots.   TSI was now at least as heavily dependent on new residential construction in western St. Tammany as it had ever been.

But that was not a bad place to be.   TSI sales in 1993 increased another 30% over 1992 sales, exceeding $3.5 million for the first time; profits were likewise the highest in company history. In 1994, sales rose another 24%, exceeding $4 million, and profits decreased only slightly.

CLOUDS ON THE HORIZON

By the end of 1994, local builders were beginning to catch up with the demand, indicating a levelling off of building activity, but at a comfortable plateau. The boom was running its course, but there certainly did not seem to be a crash in sight.

There were ways, however, in which this situation felt different from the prosperity of the early 1980s. TSI's early success was accelerated by the high-end nature of the St. Tammany housing industry; their clientele bought luxury goods, with their attendant luxurious profit margins. In the 1990's, most of the housing being built was middle-range and below; margins were skimpy, and TSI had to move a lot more material to make as much profit.

The competitive situation also felt different. The regional plumbing supply chain which had opened a branch in the market in 1991 seemed to be there to stay, despite its inability to take a significant share of business from TSI. Another chain operator was making serious noises about joining the competition in western St. Tammany.

As the market had gone a bit downscale, TSI was becoming more vulnerable to the low-price, low-service sales approach of the larger companies. The resultant discomfort was intensified by the announcement of a Home Depot being built just 2 miles south of TSI.

RELATED DEVELOPMENTS

As John Vinturella, TSI president, looked at the 1994 sales reports, he thought what a hardened pessimist he must be. Despite two record-breaking years in a row, he was feeling burned out on business, and dreading the prospect of facing another economic cycle, mild though it seemed.

From 1986 to 1988, Vinturella had worked on a personal-investment diversification program to supplement the one he directed at TSI. He seeded the startup of a microbrewery, and then sold his stake to seed a "cajun food" manufacturer. He bought a computer-consulting firm and merged it with the software company used by TSI. He and his brothers opened a quick-oil-change franchise in New Orleans. Vinturella was positioned to prosper when the area economy recovered.

While the area economy had found bottom in 1987, it merely bounced along that bottom for the next few years. Vinturella overestimated the pace of recovery, and experienced another "crash," this time in his personal finances, beginning in 1990. Investments from ten years earlier had started to become drains on cash. The recent investments were taking longer to reach profitability than projected.

Vacancies in the TSI building were causing tremendous strains in making mortgage payments. An orderly shutdown of these ventures was begun, climaxing in 1992 when Vinturella returned his building to the bank.

Because of his personal financial reverses, TSI had become Vinturella's only significant asset. The thought of cashing out entered his mind; were he to sell now, at a peak, he would probably be able to live off the proceeds for life.

DECISION TIME

From his early 1995 perspective, Vinturella observes that he is little-needed at TSI and that suits him fine. At 52 years old, he is ready to formalize his separation from the business. Ron is also 52, and should be around for 15 more years. Scott, 30 years old, is progressing nicely in the business, and showing leadership potential.

In 1993, Vinturella's outside income exceeded his TSI income. In 1994, outside income fell off a bit, increasing his reliance on the TSI draw. A moderately large consulting contract was expected in early 1995 that would support him through the summer, but nothing certain for the rest of the year yet.

Vinturella figured that investing the proceeds of the sale of the company would provide as much income as he was drawing from the company now, without any of the worries of the business. He enjoyed his outside activities far more than his TSI duties.

He reached into his file drawer, and pulled out the folder marked "Selling the Business." It contained a letter from a business brokerage service offering to list his business for sale, and a prospectus on an electrical supply house for sale that he thought could serve as a model for his listing (copies attached).

But on the other hand ...

 **PUT YOURSELF IN THEIR SHOES**

- Is now a good time to sell, or do prospective buyers see the same danger signs that Vinturella sees? Should he approach the firm currently considering entering the market? Can he get that firm and his current competitor into a "bidding war?"

- Are the danger signs real or imagined? Is Vinturella just getting "gun-shy" from his earlier reverses? Would a levelling off at this sales volume adversely affect TSI's profitability?

- Were some of Vinturella's recent decisions those of a short-termer? Was the reversal of the diversification program short-sighted? Has the market matured to the point where TSI has lost the competitive advantage of being the small, independent, locally owned firm?

- Is it smart for Vinturella to consider selling now, when his alternate sources of income are not yielding much, or should he wait until his other pursuits prove more profitable? Is it fair for him to continue to draw a substantial salary? What do you see happening to TSI's market value if he waits a year or two to offer it for sale?

- Assuming that the business might appraise for a million dollars, how much might Vinturella realize from its sale? What kind of income might that provide for life? What would the investment options be? Does he owe anything to his children?

- What are Vinturella's real reasons for considering a sale of the business? Could his sense of no longer being needed be driving it, or is it for business reasons? How might Ron and Scott react if he brought them into discussing the possibility?

- Were Vinturella to decide not to sell; are there any dangers in prolonging the current situation? Might other employees perceive it as a disinterested leader, caretaker manager, not-yet-ready successor designate? Do they care? Is it an accurate perception? How might customers and suppliers view the situation? What about competitors?

- Can Vinturella really be the company leader on a one-day-a-week schedule? Even with his loss of interest? Are there any actions he can take, short of selling, to pass on the leadership of TSI? Can a non-owner manager be a leader? How soon can Scott take over? When should he? What are the criteria?

TIME OUT! YOUR COACH SAYS

What are the common strategic options in growing a business? How do we choose between them? What are the drawbacks of the options you may choose?

Why would a business owner not pursue a growth strategy? Will your business still be viable if you decide not to pursue growth? How does this affect your company vision and objectives?

Parting Thought

This book was written with the purpose of supporting you as an entrepreneur. Remind yourself of the title. Where is the entrepreneur within you and how long will you leave your aspirations, ability and dreams hidden inside while living an uninspired life. In this book we aim to support you in your development as an entrepreneur and business owner, believing in your dreams and providing you with the tools to make them a reality. But you also need to keep in mind that there are millions of great business ideas out there, there are many a most brilliant idea that's still lying on shelf and probably will do forever. A good idea is only the start of creating a successful flourishing business. This book has started to introduce the many other aspects there are to a winning business and it's up to you use your resourcefulness, resilience, networks and natural ability to add the rest.

Every business starts with dream. It is the brave and daring entrepreneur that becomes the dream and sees it come true.

To your success

Ben Botes & John Vinturella

Resources

Web Resources http://www.ryie.com/resources/

Podcasts http://www.ryie.com/podcasts/

About the Authors

John B. Vinturella, Ph.D., has written books on entrepreneurship and small-business management (see Amazon.com) and maintains sites on entrepreneurship (jbv.com), Internet marketing (ryie.com) and personal finance (semi-retirement.com). Dr. Vinturella also maintains blogs on business (secondfortune.blogspot.com) and on New Orleans' recovery from hurricane Katrina (nobulletin.blogspot.com). Your comments and suggestions are always welcome (jbv@jbv.com).

Ben Botes MBA is an entrepreneur, management consultant, executive coach and one of the UK's new leading thinkers on the coaching of entrepreneurs and small business leadership. Owning his first business at age 24 Ben has started and run business in the call center, transportation, consulting and coaching industries. Ben has worked with and supported entrepreneurs on four continents and is the founder of a web portal for 1st time business owners (www.my1stbusiness.com) and the co-founder of a national entrepreneurial support network in South Africa (www.sabusinesshub.co.za). Read Bens Blog, viva small business, at www.sabusinesshub.com/weblog

Printed in the United States
87724LV00003BA/261/A